GIANTS OF THE SEA

CREATURES OF FASCINATION

Andrew Cleave

LONGMEADOW
PRESS

This 1993 edition published by Longmeadow Press,
201 High Ridge Road, Stamford, CT 06904

This book was designed and produced by
Todtri Productions Limited
P.O. Box 20058
New York, NY 10023–1482

Printed and Bound in Singapore

Library of Congress Catalog Card Number 93–77387

ISBN 0–681–45321–4

Author: Andrew Cleave

Producer: Robert M. Tod
Book Designer: Mark Weinberg
Editor: Mary Forsell
Photo Editor: Natasha Milne
Design Associate: Jackie Skroczky

TABLE OF CONTENTS

INTRODUCTION

Truly, even to a thoughtless mind, this great ocean is enough to set one a-thinking.
—**J.E. Taylor**, *FGS Half Hours at the Sea-side*, 1872

Humans have always been fascinated by the sea. Its vastness, its terrifying power during a storm, its riches of food, and its many curiosities have always drawn people to it. Since man first learned to fashion simple vessels from wood, reeds, and animal skins the seas have also been a means of traveling around the globe. The first sailors learned to make use of the winds and ocean currents and developed skills of navigation.

They passed on these skills to succeeding generations, who improved on their knowledge by further explorations and longer journeys. They ventured farther and farther in search of food and marveled at the way in which year after year the seas gave up their riches. From time to time strange creatures were caught or tantalizing glimpses were seen of curious animals, the likes of which were never seen on land. Stories were told of enormous creatures as large as or larger than ships. Perhaps some of these were exaggerated in the telling and retelling of the stories and the creatures grew in size and ferocity over the years. Some have become part of the folklore of ancient peoples; the stories of classical Greece are filled with references to the seas and their mysteries. The Bible, too, has its share of references to the seas, most notably such stories as Jonah and the whale and the parting of the Red Sea by Moses.

For many centuries man lived in harmony with the sea. Its riches were used but not exploited. Fish were taken at levels that enabled populations to regenerate, and many species remained out of reach of the current fishing techniques by living in remote parts of the oceans, by inhabiting the deepest places, or by being too swift to be caught.

The great whales were also hunted, yet in most cases this was at a level that could be sustained. Slow-moving, surface-active species like the Biscayan right whale were hunted to the verge of extinction, but such fast-swimming, open-ocean species as the blue whale and the minke whale were largely unaffected.

The seas in the polar regions were so remote that for many centuries they remained largely unexplored and were the last truly wild places on earth.

Before the coming of the Industrial Age in Europe and later in North America the worst form of pollution to reach the seas was human waste from large cities on the coast or near estuaries. This was to change as populations increased and industrial processes became more complex. Mining, iron smelting, chemical production, and even agriculture all contributed to the flow of undesirable materials poured into the seas from the land. The volume of waste poured into the seas increased. At the same time, the nature of the waste changed. Far more unpleasant chemicals found their way into the seas, and some passed through the food chain by way of plants, shrimp, and fish to find their way back to the top predators, humans themselves.

Improvements in industrial processes and agriculture led to further increases in human populations, creating an even greater demand for food. Better navigational techniques, stronger vessels, and the coming of steam power enabled ships to travel farther and faster and stay at sea for longer periods. Gradually, even the most remote parts of the deepest oceans came within reach of man's ingenuity and became vulnerable to his potentially damaging influence. Improved fishing methods took their toll of the traditional food species like the herring and cod, and the great whales were hunted relentlessly. Entire food chains were interrupted as both predator and prey species were taken.

With the coming of oil and the internal combustion engine, the vastness of the oceans seemed to shrink still further; ships became larger and faster, and the volume of waste poured into the seas increased to dangerous levels. Ships carrying deadly cargoes of oil foundered on reefs, spilling their contents into the seas; millions of seabirds met their deaths with their feathers clogged with black oil. Those that survived faced the problem of competing with fishermen for dwindling supplies of food. For those that were successful in finding food, another, more insidious threat confronted them: It was so likely that their food had been contaminated with the poisons that had poured into the seas for so long that there was a strong possibility that their eggs would not hatch or their offspring would fail to develop.

The warning signs had been seen for a long time as fishermen reported reduced catches and greater difficulty in finding sufficient fish. Populations of seabirds on breeding islands crashed as their food supplies ran out. The great whales came close to extinction as the slaughter continued, and even the most die-hard whaling nations agreed to accept reduced quotas. Public awareness was aroused by reports of declining populations of sea creatures; bathing beaches were declared unsafe due to contamination of the water, and publicized oil spills alerted the public to what was happening to the seas, which make up seventy-five percent of the planet's surface.

We began to take a fresh look at the seas and our relationship with them. We could no longer look on the seas as a vast and bottomless pit into which all manner of waste substances could be dumped without any ill effect. It became more and more apparent that things had gone seriously wrong and that urgent conservation measures had to be adopted in order to halt the decline of endangered species and to prevent any further extinctions. The future of the human race was also in the balance, and the urgent conservation measures needed to save species like the whales would also benefit future generations of humans.

Now the seas are regarded as a vital and integral part of the life of our planet. Indeed, we now understand that the whole basis of life on earth is affected by the oceans. The very climate of this planet is governed by the oceans, and our food, the air we breathe, and the waste we produce (which must be carefully disposed of) all depend on a healthy marine environment.

THE SURFACE OF THE SEA

And on the calm, cool nights how often have I stood on the deck of a ship watching with wonder and awe the stars overhead, and the sea-fire below, especially in the silvery wake of the vessel, where often suddenly appear globes of soft and lambent light, given out perhaps from the surface of some large Medusa.

—Sir John Lubbock, *The Beauties of Nature*, 1892

For most of us, the surface of the sea is the only part of this watery environment with which we ever come into contact. For many of us, this is enough. What lies below the surface remains a mystery, and we are content to leave it that way.

Even though we may never venture below the surface or see what lives there, the surface itself provides plenty of interest. This is the area where we see the marine creatures and where some of them may even come to look at us. At the surface the water is at its warmest. Because of the water's contact with the air, it has the highest levels of oxygen. The turbulence of the waves leads to a constant aeration of the upper layers of the sea, enriching the water with the oxygen essential for the respiration of fish. This is also where the light intensity is the brightest, so plant growth is most abundant here.

The surface of the sea is the place where debris from the land and from rivers may be found; flotsam and jetsam from ships passing over the surface mingle with the sea's own debris in the form of storm-damaged seaweeds and the dead bodies of sea creatures.

Billions of microscopic organisms live at the surface, unseen and undetected by the larger creatures passing over it. Microscopic plants, single-celled members of the algae, a large and important plant family, use the bright light of the sun, trapping its energy to make their food. Sunlight alone does not support them, however, for they also need minerals to help build their tissues. Ocean currents sweeping up from the deep

ocean troughs bring nutrients from the depths that the microscopic plants can utilize.

When conditions are suitable, the microscopic plants can grow and multiply to such an extent that they color the seawater green, cutting out all light to the depths below. The richer the green color in the water, the more abundant the algae. In places where microscopic algae grow in profusion, the microscopic animals that feed on them will also increase in numbers. These tiny animals graze on the single-celled plants, and in turn they may form dense clouds, further obscuring the light in the water below.

Some of these microscopic organisms can move independently, but most of them simply drift at the mercy of the wind and tides. Ocean currents carry them over great distances, and those that reach unsuitable places die and fall to the bed of the sea, adding to the already rich store of nutrients lying on the bottom. These drifting organisms are collectively known as plankton, from the Greek word *planktos*, which means "drifting" or "wandering."

Although minute and among the smallest of living things, they are often beautiful to look at, as they exhibit a bewildering array of shapes, forms, and colors. Some have delicate shells formed from chalk or silica, and these help to form deep layers of silt on the seabed as their dead bodies accumulate over long periods. They may be tiny, but collectively they are of immense importance to the giants of the sea, who all, in some way or other, depend on them for food.

With such a wealth of microscopic food available, an entire food web can develop, culminating in the largest creatures of all: the great whales. Humans, too, are directly affected by these tiny creatures: Our favored food species, including herring, capelin, and mackerel, feed on smaller organisms. Tiny shrimp and small fish that feed on microscopic creatures are in turn preyed on by larger fish, which may be eaten by larger fish still or even whales. Some of the largest whales feed directly on the planktonic organisms by swimming slowly through the surface layers, filtering huge quantities of water to obtain enough of the tiny creatures to sustain them. This is more efficient than feeding on the fish, which eat the plankton, as they waste less energy by simply grazing than they would if they had to pursue fast-swimming fish.

Not all seas are rich in plankton; where the water is crystal clear and the seabed can be seen, there can be no plankton present. This is often the case in tropical regions, where although there may be plenty of sunlight and warm water, there is a lack of dissolved nutrients in the water. The seas in such places could be described as a biological desert, for there is no scope here for the plankton feeders to find their food. Some of the great whales, like the humpback, migrate from the cold but productive feeding grounds of the Arctic to warmer waters off the Bahamas and Hawaii, where their young are born. The warm water is more suitable for the birth of the whale calves, and they feed on their mothers' milk while they remain in the area.

The adults do not feed for several months while they are at the breeding grounds. Instead they use the vast store of energy in their thick blubber layers to sustain them. When the young are strong enough to make the long migration, the adults return with them to the good feeding grounds in the colder waters of the north.

The most productive areas for plankton are where cold currents well up from the ocean depths, carrying nutrients from the seabed to the surface sunlight. The combination of light and nutrients encourages the growth of billions of microscopic plants, which in turn feed on microscopic animals. These are then preyed on by larger organisms, such as shrimp and fish. This type of food chain often occurs in polar regions, and here there may be huge concentrations of seabirds feeding on fish nourished by the plankton, together with high populations of other fish eaters, such as seals and whales.

Filter-feeding mollusks also rely on plankton, and they support populations of large mammals like the walrus, also an abundant species in the colder regions of the Arctic.

More temperate regions such as the Gulf of Maine in America are also highly productive areas for plankton, but even on the equator where the Galapagos Islands rise up out of the deep Pacific Ocean, upwellings of the cold Antarctic current produce good blooms of algae. These plankton-rich areas have traditionally provided good fishing for both humans and marine creatures, and it is here that many of the giants of the sea can be found feeding directly on the plankton or on the larger species, which are themselves plankton feeders.

The Galapagos Islands are noted for their large colonies of seabirds and sea lions, including many species that would normally be found in much colder regions instead of directly on the equator.

They are all sustained by the plankton, itself nourished by the upwelling cold currents.

Several drifting organisms utilize winds that blow across the surface of the sea. The deadly Portuguese man-of-war has an air-filled sail that it extends above the surface to catch air currents. As the animal's long, stinging tentacles stream out below it in the water, its sail catches the wind and spreads out over great distances, catching tiny organisms as it travels. This animal's greatest danger is coming too close to land; once driven into shallow water or onto a beach, it is quite unable to free itself and reach deeper water again. The smaller sailors and the beautiful violet sea snail also catch the winds with their small sails and bubble floats and cover huge distances at the sea's surface.

The surface of the sea may become contaminated by oil spillages; it is then a far less hospitable place for marine life. Birds can no longer dive for fish or surface safely for air without becoming coated with a thick layer of oil. The oxygen essential to animals for their respiration cannot reach the water through the surface film, and the light required by the plants as an energy source is prevented from passing through.

SEA SERPENT OF HANS EGIDIUS.

THE DEPTHS OF THE SEA

*The Great Deep! What a world of sublimity,
of countless wealth, of awful power! Let the great
deep share man's thought, and it shall inspire
his admiration, his wonder, his awe.*

—Anonymous, *Half Hours In The Deep, 1898*

Light only penetrates for a short distance below the surface of the sea, so in the depths of the ocean there is an all-enveloping, inky darkness, broken only by the flashing lights of phosphorescent plankton or bioluminescent fish. Near the surface, where some light filters through, countless species of large fish swim, some in shoals, some in solitary isolation. Many are silvery below and have blue-green colorings on their flanks and upper surfaces to help them blend in with the pale green light that reaches them during the day.

Fish of the open ocean are streamlined and swift; they must pursue their prey in a place where there is nowhere to hide and must somehow avoid being captured themselves. Large jellyfish drift in the currents just below the surface, trailing deadly tentacles that can ensnare fish. Strange comb jel-lies, so transparent that they are almost invisible, move slowly with the current, their elegant but lethal feeding tentacles flowing behind them.

Into this underwater world come the air-breathing whales. The strange, bulbous-head-ed sperm whale dives deep in pursuit of giant squid, its favorite prey. In these cold, dark depths it must locate its prey by sonar, or echo-location, for its tiny eyes will be of no use here. The small cookie-cutter shark irritates the large whales by following them into the depths and biting circular chunks of skin out of their flanks and fins. Although it is only a small fish, it shows no fear in attacking a creature hundreds of times larger than itself. Many whales bear the characteristic circular scars of this small, bold shark.

Beaked whales and pilot whales also dive deep down in search of squid, and the water may res-onate with their call as they use their own sonar to find prey in total darkness. Larger ocean-going sharks, like the blue and porbeagle, cruise silently through the depths in search of prey. They may take injured fish or attack marine mammals. Their coloring suits their blue-green environ-ment perfectly, and it is only when they approach the surface that they are noticed.

The enormous ocean sunfish—which can attain a length of 10 feet (3.1 meters) and weigh in excess of 2 tons (1.8 metric tons)—is at home here in the open sea. Once it was thought that this oddly shaped fish enjoyed basking at the surface, absorbing the warmth of the sun, but it is now clear that individuals at the surface are unwell or under stress. Their true habitat is the deep ocean, where they feed on small fish and squid.

THE SEABED

The bed of the ocean resembles in a great degree the surface of the earth. It has its mountains and its valleys, its plains and deserts, its various kinds of rocks and soils.

—Samuel Octavius Gray, *British Seaweeds*, 1867

Only in very shallow seas and in very clear water does any light reach the seabed. For the most part, the seabed is a place of total darkness. This inky blackness is broken at times, however, for even here there is life; many of the strange creatures that live in the depths can emit their own light. Ghostly flashing and flickering lights can be seen emanating from the many creatures living deep below the surface.

The great wealth of life in the upper parts of the oceans produces a huge quantity of material in the form of organic waste matter. The excreta of birds, mammals, and fish, the dead bodies of these creatures, and the spent remains of billions of microscopic creatures all eventually fall to the bed of the sea in the form of a constant "snowstorm" of tiny particles. When it reaches the seabed, this waste material adds to the dense accumulation of debris already present, which makes this habitat a productive feeding place for scavenging organisms.

In relatively shallow seas, such as the North Sea, and on continental shelf areas, this debris-filled seabed is a highly productive environment. The rich silt is laden with organic matter, which is the basis of an important series of food chains forming a complex food web, with man and the great whales as major predators. The scavengers and filter feeders on the seabed feed directly on the organic matter and are in turn preyed on by such predators as crabs, squid, and larger fish.

The enormous halibut spends its life on the seabed, feeding on other fish and large crustaceans. This is an unusual species of fish that lies on its side, unlike the skates and rays, which are flattened from top to bottom and rest on their undersides. Burrowing worms, crabs, and mollusks all live here in homes they excavate for themselves and attract larger predators down to feed on them. In shallow seas the gray whale and the walrus may dive down to search for buried clams, while in deeper water the anglerfish lies in wait for an unsuspecting fish to come close to its huge mouth.

THE CORAL REEF

Thus do we see the soft and gelatinous body of a polyps, through the agency of the vital laws, conquering the great mechanical power of the waves of an ocean which neither the art of man nor the inanimate works of nature could successfully resist.

—Charles Darwin, *The Voyage Of The Beagle*, 1845

The warm, clear waters of the tropics provide the perfect conditions for the growth of coral and the formation of a remarkable feat of nature, the coral reef. Countless millions of tiny organisms, both plants and animals, together form one of the most complex ecosystems in the world—a vast collection of microscopic plants and animals creating the basis of a whole community of incredible variety and often stunning beauty. The reef-building corals—soft-bodied animals encased in chalky skeletons—provide the structure of the reef, which is then colonized by a bewildering variety of plants, crustaceans, starfish, mollusks, and fish, all vying with one other to be more colorful or more perfectly adapted to life in this complex environment.

A reef-building coral is a small invertebrate animal that begins life as a tiny, free-swimming larva, part of the plankton carried along in the ocean currents. If the tiny larva avoids being eaten by the many plankton feeders swimming in the oceans, it will try to settle on a suitable hard surface, preferably in a warm, shallow place where there is plenty of sunlight. Once settled, the larva grows into a tiny polyp with a mouth surrounded by tentacles. It will secrete a hard external skeleton around itself, consisting mainly of calcium carbonate, or chalk.

As the polyp grows, it divides to form two new polyps rather than increasing in size. This is a form of asexual reproduction that enables the

Tall pillar corals grow above the smaller species of coral on the reef and are better able to capture tiny food particles as they are carried past in the current. They are unable to grow as tall and straight as this in very strong currents.

numbers of individuals to increase rapidly under favorable conditions. Each tiny polyp has its own skeleton, and these combine to form the basis of the reef. The individual polyps all feed separately but are part of the same colony. Eventually the original polyps die, but their skeletons remain. As more and more individuals are formed by the division or budding of existing corals, the colony increases in size, building on the firm base provided by the original colonizers. The coral colony will grow upward and outward. Eventually, the skeletons of the first coral polyps will be completely hidden and submerged. In large and long-established reefs, the coral skeletons deep inside form a solid, rocklike structure—the result of modifications by pressure and the addition of dissolved minerals.

Several hundred species of coral have been identified in the world's reefs. Some are widespread and abundant, while others are more rare and specialized, but they are all built to the same basic plan.

Sponges are primitive animals with simple bodies. They live by filtering seawater to extract food particles. This brown tube sponge grows on reefs and wrecks in the Caribbean.

The finely branched sea fan spreads itself out across the current in order to trap food particles as they are swept by. This delicate and slow-growing species suffers from overcollecting and is now only common in protected areas.

The large, overlapping lobes of the plate coral, found on the Great Barrier Reef, provide excellent hiding places for many species of reef fish and crabs. The coral itself becomes colonized by other coral species and small algae, forming an important microhabitat on the reef.

In daylight the brain coral shows its hard skeleton, as the soft polyps are retracted inside the coral. At night the living polyps extend their soft, feeding tentacles, giving the coral its brainlike appearance.

A diver explores the colorful world of a coral reef in the tropical Pacific. If divers look but do not touch, the reefs will survive. However, if they treat the reefs as collecting grounds, the beautiful, slow-growing corals will disappear. Care should be taken not to snap off brittle branches of coral colonies, which may have taken many years to form.

The massive shell of a giant clam has been colonized by hard corals. Only the mantle of the clam is left exposed, enabling it to continue feeding.

The green, leaflike lobes of the lettuce coral of the Red Sea give it the appearance of a plant. In reality, it is a colonial animal in a hard, calcareous skeleton. Microscopic algae create the green coloration.

Following page:

The flattened branches of an elkhorn coral spread out above the smaller corals, competing with them for space and food. The flattened branches most resemble the antlers of the moose, not the North American elk.

Corals must live in shallow seas because their tissues contain millions of microscopic plants that require light in order to produce their food by photosynthesis. Even the clearest tropical water absorbs some of the light that passes through it, so that below a depth of about 165 feet (50 meters) there is not enough light energy to be useful to plants. Corals cannot tolerate exposure to the air, so the upper limit to their colonization is the lowest point to which the tides fall—the extreme low-water mark of spring tides. No coral polyp can survive in a free-floating state, as it must be anchored in order to start building its chalky skeleton. These three restrictions limit the corals to warm, clear waters of less than 165 feet (50 meters) in depth filled with firm rocks.

There are some coral species that can survive in water where light levels are very low. These live solely on the food they trap for themselves and do not rely on the microscopic plants to help them. These corals grow well in deep gulleys, where there is a constant current of water sweeping past containing a supply of food particles. They do not thrive in still water, where sediment collects.

Coral reefs often form in a ring around volcanic islands. The island may be eroded away and sink back into the sea, but the coral reef, being a complex collection of living organisms, is able to continue growing. If the sea level rises, the coral can grow upward. If parts of the reef are worn away by storms, they will eventually be replaced by regrowth. There are many examples in the tropical Pacific of atolls, or rings of coral surrounding a shallow lagoon that once had an island rising from its center.

A soft coral lacks the hard, calcareous skeleton of the reef-building corals. The many fine tentacles of the numerous polyps are extended in order to trap plankton.

At night, many tiny polyps emerge from their hard, protective coral skeleton to feed on microscopic plants and animals. Each ring of tentacles surrounds a tiny mouth. If it catches a food item, the ring of tentacles close over and push it toward the mouth.

The staghorn coral of the Caribbean is a fragile species, easily snapped if touched. It grows best in sheltered conditions and provides plenty of hiding places for fish.

The open siphon of this sea squirt indicates that it is drawing in seawater. Once it has taken in the water, the siphon closes and the water passes over tissues, which remove food particles before the water passes out again through the other siphon.

The tentacles of these Indonesian tube corals show the many stinging cells used to immobilize prey when they are touched.

A barrel sponge releases a cloud of reproductive cells into the water. Free-swimming larvae eventually settle on a firm surface and begin to develop the many types of cells needed to form a new sponge.

A cluster of blue sea squirts filter-feeds on a reef, surrounded by multicolored coral debris. Sea squirts are abundant organisms in places where there is a current to provide a constant supply of food and oxygen.

Some lagoons become deep as sediment collects in their centers. The sediment smothers the coral, which can no longer grow. As the sea level rises still farther, the central lagoon deepens and the surrounding ring of coral reef grows upward. The smallest of all coral reefs are formed when a few individual coral colonies come together to create a small patch. These grow upward until stopped by the sea level, at which point they grow outward. The center of the colony gradually dies away, leaving a shallow, saucerlike depression, but the micro-atoll continues to grow outward for some time, until it is several meters in diameter.

Several micro-atolls may come together to form a much larger structure, such as a barrier reef. Barrier reefs form in shallow water off the coast of larger land masses. The Great Barrier Reef of Australia is a classic example. Nearly 1,250 miles (2,000 kilometers) long, it supports countless millions of plants and animals and is one of the wonders of the natural world.

There are many species of coral living in any reef, and in some particularly rich reefs over two hundred different species have been identified. Some of these are the important reef builders, which are long lived and form solid structures, while others are colonizers, able to live on the reef as long as they receive some support and protection from other corals. Some corals are very delicate and grow only in more sheltered places, while others prefer exposed situations. Corals appear to grow best on the edges of the reef, particularly on the seaward edge, where they receive some exposure to wave action; this keeps them supplied with food in the form of plankton and plenty of oxygen for respira-

A delicate and much-branched sea fan on an overhang on a tropical Pacific reef indicates a gentle current; in strong currents the fan seems swept to one side. Spread out in the water in this manner, it is able to capture minute creatures carried by in the water.

The barrel sponges of the tropical Pacific are among the largest of their kind. The soft body tissues are strengthened by millions of tiny spicules formed of silica. The body surface is covered with minute pores, through which water is drawn to be filtered, and it then leaves through the large, central siphon.

The brilliantly colored Gulf star is a common starfish of the eastern Pacific from Mexico to Peru. Its spiny skin and bright coloration are good defenses against predators.

Sea squirts, or ascidians, are simple-looking, saclike animals, but they have a complex larva with a simple nerve chord, making them closely related to animals with backbones. They are filter feeders, drawing in water through a siphon.

tion. Waste products are also carried away easily.

In addition to the great variety of corals, a host of other animals lives on reefs. Many are filter feeders, drawing in a constant stream of seawater. Sponges are among the most primitive of animals, but they can develop quite large colonies in favorable conditions. The porous surface of a sponge is made up of thousands of tiny holes through which water is sucked in by special feeding cells. The pores all eventually connect to a larger opening. This expels filtered water along with any waste products.

Some sponges are brilliantly colored, adding to the overall attractiveness of reefs. The color is usually due to the presence of microscopic plants living inside the sponge tissues—the same arrangement that occurs in many of the corals. This partnership, between a simple animal and a

The basket seastar of Australia has unusual, multibranched arms. It actually has five arms, like all other starfish, but the many branches create the impression of many more. Starfish can attain sizes of over 3 feet (91 centimeters).

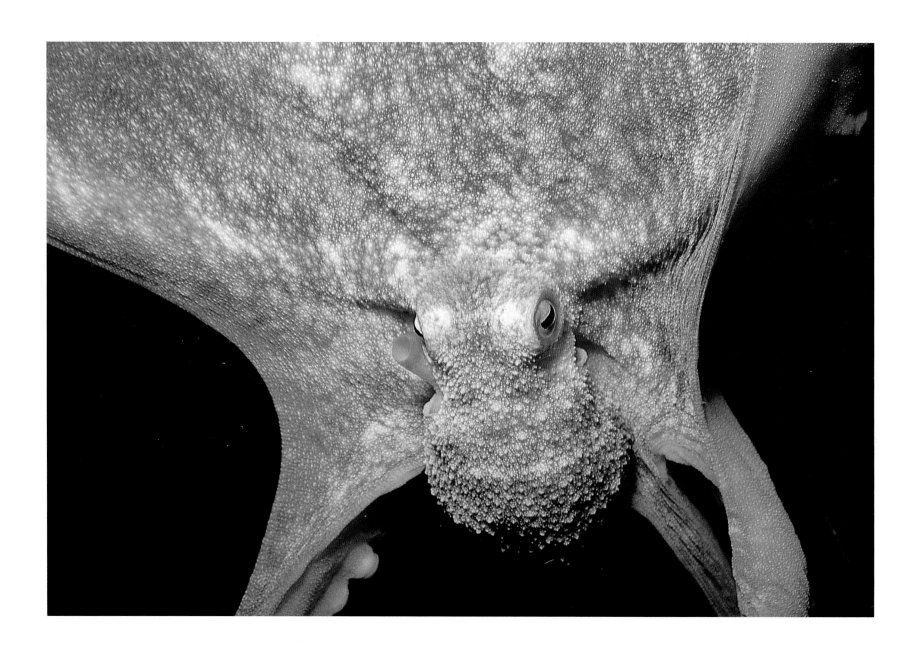

The octopus is a complex mollusk that has no shell at all. Its baglike body is very flexible, and the eight tentacles, capable of rapid movements, are joined at the base by a web of skin. An octopus has very good eyesight, and its reflexes are quick enough for it to be able to catch fast-moving prey like crabs.

simple plant, is beneficial to both parties and is known as symbiosis. It is a surprisingly widespread phenomenon in the living world, especially in an environment as complex as the coral reef. The cleaner fish, such as the remoras—which pick parasites from the body of a larger fish or snatch scraps as it feeds—are performing a useful service to their host fish, while at the same time receiving some protection themselves.

Another type of filter-feeding organism on the reef is the sea squirt. This looks like a primitive animal, but is in fact quite complex. In its early stages it produces a tadpolelike larva with a simple nerve cord, making it a close relative of animals with backbones. Sea squirts draw in seawater through one opening, or siphon, pass it through their gut and remove any edible materials, and then pass the filtered water out through the other siphon. They are often found in clusters attached to

An octopus withdraws to its lair, a crevice in a coral reef, where it may remain hidden for hours. Its main prey is crabs, which it grabs with a lightning strike by one or more sucker-lined tentacles.

The giant, or red hermit, crab is the largest species found on Caribbean coasts. Its red claws are covered with rough granules, and the right claw is larger than the left. Occupying the empty shell of a mollusk, such as a queen conch, the hermit crab protects the soft tissues of its body by withdrawing into the shell. When the crab outgrows its home, it must find a new and larger shell.

A cluster of horseshoe crabs on Sanibel Island, Florida, during the spring mass-mating ritual. When the water temperature reaches 70 degrees F (21 degrees C), they leave the sea and attract hungry gulls, shorebirds, fish, crabs, and curious human onlookers. Plenty survive, and the females lay masses of blue-gray eggs in the sand.

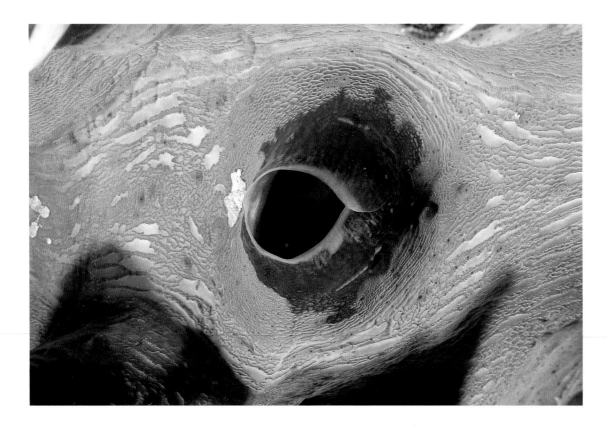

The long legs of a spider crab help it reach food in crevices and awkward places. At the end of its first pair of long legs are fine pincers, which it uses to pick up small pieces of food. The long walking legs have no pincers.

Giant clams are filter feeders, drawing a current of water into the shell through a siphon, pictured here. This water is passed over the mantle tissues, where food particles are removed, and then passed out through a second siphon.

A horseshoe crab rests on the shell beach of Cape Sable, Florida. In spring, the deepwater crabs migrate to the shore to mate and lay eggs on the high-tide line.

Light-sensitive eye spots are located in the mantle folds of the giant clam. If a shadow falls across them, the clam responds by clamping the two valves of its shell together with powerful muscles. The clam is strong enough to firmly grip, and even break, a human limb.

hard corals and are sometimes beautifully colored. Some live concealed in caves or under rocks, but many of them live out on the reef, where they can obtain a constant supply of food.

One of the largest denizens of the reef, and a giant by any standards, is the giant clam. As with many other reef dwellers, this huge mollusk lives by filter feeding. The clam opens its enormous shell and draws water in through a feeding siphon. Inside the hard shell is the living tissue. The part that is visible is known as the mantle, and this is often brightly colored, once again the result of the presence of millions of microscopic plants.

Giant clams thrive in sunny places, as the microscopic plants in their tissues require light energy. Embedded in the mantle are light-sensitive eye spots: If a shadow falls across the clam, indicating a possible threat, it can quickly respond and close up its shell. When the two halves of the shell snap

The giant clam's shell can grow to be around 4 feet (1.2 meters) long, making it the largest bivalve mollusk in the seas. This is a common reef species in the Indo-Pacific region. The living clam may weigh as much as 165 pounds (74 kilograms), while the massive shell can weigh over 400 pounds (180 kilograms). They were once used as hip baths in China.

Following page:

The colorful folds of the mantle, or living tissue, inside the gaping shell of this giant clam contain microscopic algae. As the sun shines on the clam, the algae absorb carbon dioxide and release oxygen, thus helping the clam in its respiration.

Even by the colorful standards of a tropical reef, the lionfish is a gaudy creature. Its color-banded body and waving spines and fin rays make it one of the most conspicuous inhabitants of the reef.

together, the force is strong enough to break a human leg. Divers are well advised not to tempt their luck and get stuck inside a clam. There are tales of people walking over a reef at low tide and inadvertently stepping into the open shell of a clam partly concealed in the coral. In such cases, the valves close up, trapping the unfortunate person.

Starfish are spiny-skinned animals related to sea urchins and sea cucumbers. They feed on mollusks and sometimes live by scavenging. Common on some reefs, they have five arms, but they do not use them for walking. Beneath the arms are rows of tube feet, suckerlike structures filled with water. These can be extended and retracted in a rhythmic way, which pulls the starfish along. The tube feet are capable of exerting quite a strong grip, so the starfish can pull on the two halves of the shell of small mollusk and wrench them apart to feed on the contents.

Although small in size, the lionfish packs a mighty punch, as its venom can cause severe pain and discomfort to a human victim. The lionfish shows a natural curiosity toward divers, and they are well advised to give it a wide berth!

One of the larger scorpion fish, the lionfish possesses thirteen spines on its back, each with a venomous sac at its base. If any other fish makes contact with the spine, a lethal dose of venom is injected.

A blue spiny lobster walks across a colorful section of the bed of the Sea of Cortez. It usually hides by day, emerging to feed at night under cover of darkness. This is a popular delicacy, and some populations have suffered badly from exploitation by fishermen.

Many types of crabs and lobsters inhabit reefs, and these are often as colorful as the other reef dwellers. The attractive red coral crab is one of the brightest and also one of the most prized by collectors. Its nocturnal habits make it difficult to see, as for most of the day it hides in crevices in the reef. Most crabs and lobsters feed by scavenging; there is always a ready supply of food, and they rarely need to travel far to find enough. If they do venture out of their hiding places, they are likely to become a meal for a large grouper.

The brilliantly colored corals and other inhabitants of the reefs have long attracted the attentions of collectors. In some primitive communities, shells and corals are used as jewelry and currency and sometimes are fashioned into simple implements. Today there is an increasing tendency to collect coral for decorating homes or selling as curiosities. For such a slow-growing organisms as the coral,

this is disastrous. They cannot replenish themselves quickly enough to keep up with collectors' activities. Shells are also collected in large numbers and exported around the world, and many reefs are now greatly impoverished, as many of their most colorful and conspicuous inhabitants have been removed.

Some reefs have been declared marine nature reserves and are strictly protected, such as on the coasts of Costa Rica and Kenya, for example, and here visitors are welcome to look, but are encouraged to leave things as they find them. Snorkeling and traveling over the reef in a glass-bottomed boat are offered as ways of viewing this fascinating world, and visitors have the satisfaction of knowing that after they have left, the reef and its inhabitants will still be there to delight other visitors.

A full-grown spiny lobster can reach a length of 2 feet (61 centimeters) and looks very fierce when it extends its legs and antennae. On closer examination, it becomes clear that it lacks the powerful pincers and pointed rostrum between the eyes of the true lobsters, but its spiny carapace is a good defense against predators.

The long tentacles of the Portuguese man-of-war drift through the water below the float and ensnare fish. The body of this complex organism consists of a collection of polyps, some designed to catch food and others to digest it; still others form reproductive cells. The sting from the tentacles, even when detached and washed up on a beach, is extremely painful to human skin.

The coral crab is one of the many colorful species found on the reefs fringing the Red Sea. It spends much of its time hiding among coral debris, blending in well with its surroundings. This crab emerges at night to seek food.

*Jellyfish, like this **Cyanea** species, should be avoided by swimmers, as they can inflict severe stings on human skin. The thick mane of stinging tentacles means certain death to small fish who swim too near.*

Jellyfish spend their lives drifting through the seas at the mercy of the ocean currents. Some are able to make gentle, pulsing movements to keep them near the surface, where food is plentiful. A number of species can emit a pale phosphorescent light. This South China Sea jellyfish was found off the coast of Malaysia.

A jellyfish trails its deadly tentacles through the warm waters of the Caribbean. Although most small creatures are paralyzed on contact with the stinging cells in the tentacles, there are some fish that can live among them without coming to any harm. Here they are safe from predators, and they will have scraps of food to feed on if the jellyfish catches some prey.

49

WHALES AND DOLPHINS

Thus provided both with swimming and breathing apparatus, these purely air-breathing animals wander over the wide ocean and live the lives of fish, making such good use of food which cannot be reached by land animals, or those which must keep near the shore, that we shall not be surprised to find that the whale family is a very large one.

—Arabella Buckley, *Winners in Life's Race*, 1882

The largest living creatures ever known on earth are the great whales, which still swim in the oceans today. The dinosaurs, the giant reptiles of past geological ages, have come and gone, but none of them ever rivaled the blue whale in size. At over 100 feet (30.3 meters) in length, a full-grown blue whale is a giant by any standards. These immense mammals are superbly adapted to life in the sea and live in perfect harmony with their environment. Their great size indicates the richness of the world they live in—a world that can provide sufficient food to support large populations of these fascinating creatures.

Whales and dolphins are mammals that belong to the order Cetacea; this group is further divided by biologists into two suborders. These are the Odontoceti, which includes all the toothed whales, and the Mysticeti, which includes the baleen whales. The smaller porpoises and dolphins, plus the pilots, sperm, beaked, and killer whales, are all included in the Odontoceti, while the great whales, such as the blue, fin, and humpback, are placed in the Mysticeti.

Whales are basically of two types: baleen and toothed. The baleen whales are those that lack true teeth. Instead, they have comblike, fibrous plates in their mouths. The baleen whales are the largest and include the blue, fin, right, and humpback types. The toothed whales all have

The huge mouth of the humpback whale gapes open as it lunges to the surface in pursuit of a shoal of herring or capelin. After it has broken through the surface, it will close its mouth and capture the fish, straining water out through its baleen plates.

Captured in the tranquility of an Alaskan sea, the killer, or orca, whale emerges briefly from the water.

51

As the blue whale begins a dive and lifts its tail out of the water, the massive tail stock can be seen, showing the powerful muscles the whale uses when swimming.

true teeth. Some, like the killer whale, have sets of powerful, sharp teeth set in strong jaws used for killing prey. The massive sperm whale has teeth in its lower jaw only, and some of the beaked whales have only a small number of teeth. Most of the porpoises and dolphins have a set of peglike teeth in each jaw, used for catching and holding fish.

There are eleven species of baleen whales, all of them large in size, but over sixty species of toothed whales, ranging in size from the huge sperm whale at up to 60 feet (18.2 meters) in length, down to the smallest porpoises at less than 6.5 feet (2 meters) in length.

The term "whale" is usually applied to any cetacean more than 33 feet (10 meters) long, but this is a rather artificial distinction. The term "dolphin" is now increasingly used to describe the cetaceans too small to be called whales, although some biologists still confine this term to members of the family Delphinidae. All the baleen, sperm, and beaked whales are now generally called whales, while all the remaining cetaceans, including the killer whale and pilot whales, are called dolphins.

Although they are all air-breathing mammals superbly well adapted for life in the sea and built roughly to the same body plan, they show a wide range of variations in feeding methods, size, shape, habits, and distribution, occurring in all the world's seas and oceans and feeding at all depths, from the surface to the seabed. Some, like the bottle-nosed dolphin and killer whale, are distributed worldwide and can be encountered almost anywhere at sea, while others have a more restricted range. Belugas confine themselves to the Arctic, tropical whales remain in equatorial regions, and many of the small porpoises live only in small populations in isolated bays or river mouths.

Aside from the blue whale, several of the other great whales are also built to staggering propor-

A breaching humpback whale is a thrilling sight for whale watchers. This exciting behavior, which is sometimes repeated many times, may be a form of communication, or a play activity in young whales.

The upper surface of a humpback whale's tail fluke, seen just before a dive, is all black with a notched edge, and may measure 13 feet (3.9 meters) across. This is what provides the power to swim.

A breaching whale often comes out of the water on its side, rolling onto its back halfway through the breach, but sometimes it comes up with its belly uppermost and splashes down onto its back.

The hooked dorsal fin of a female minke whale shows clearly as she prepares to dive, while her calf lunges out of the water beside her, showing its white throat and clean, straight jawline.

tions. The fin whale may reach a length of 90 feet (27.3 meters), and the rotund bowhead, right, and humpback whales, although shorter, have massive, bulky bodies and enormous heads and mouths. An elephant, the largest of the land mammals, can quite easily stand inside the mouth of a blue or fin whale. The great sperm whale, feared by the old whalers, once regularly reached lengths of up to 60 feet (18.2 meters), but ruthless hunting has resulted in much smaller average sizes.

The massive body of a whale cannot sustain itself on land. A beached whale is quite unable to move itself and return to the water, and its internal organs are in danger of being crushed by the weight of its body. In water, the whale is supported and is able to move with ease. Its skeleton is reduced to a strong spine and skull, with the front limbs modified to form flippers and the hind limbs almost completely absent. Ribs are present, but other structures—including the pelvic and pectoral girdles, which support the limbs in land-living mammals—are greatly reduced in size.

Whales are air-breathing mammals, so they must all make regular trips to the surface to empty stale air from their lungs and replenish it with fresh. This is the time when most people spot their first whale, as the air rushing out of the lungs through the blowhole makes a visible plume of vapor above the water. The "blow" of each species of whale is quite distinctive and is a useful identification feature. The great column of vapor from a blue whale is the largest, but the forked blow of a right whale, the pear-shaped blow of the humpback, and the sideways blow of the sperm whale are all easily recognized at sea.

The blow can also be heard and smelled. Some species have a very explosive blow, and in still conditions or in enclosed areas like deep fjords, the blow is often heard before being seen. The smell of a whale's breath can sometimes be detected and has been likened to a combination of fish and rotting cabbage, but it is rather an elusive scent.

When a whale dives, it must hold its breath until reaching the surface again. The blowhole closes tightly and the whale can dive without taking in any water. Some species dive for only a few minutes at a time, making frequent trips to the surface. The species that feed on plankton need not dive very deeply as their food is always fairly close to the surface and they do not need to pursue it for any length of time.

The whales that feed on squid and other deepwater species must make deeper and longer dives, and these hold the record for duration. The deep-diving whales are all toothed whales. The sperm whale, pilot whales, and the beaked whales can all stay under for long periods, commonly diving for around one hour to great depths. They seek their food in total darkness, in very cold water, and at great pressure. As they dive they reduce the blood flow to parts of the body to save oxygen and conserve heat. Their muscle tissue is able to store oxygen and accumulate respiration waste. This enables whales to expel waste through their lungs when they return to the water's surface.

The beluga has a very expansive face and a more flexible neck than most other whales, enabling it to turn its head independently of its body.

Following page:

The large, all-black, bulbous head of the long-finned pilot whale cannot be mistaken for the black-and-white killer whale. The huge head contains a structure that helps the whale echo-locate squid and fish in the darkness of deep water.

A short-finned pilot whale surfaces in the Indian Ocean after a deep dive in search of its favorite food, squid. Its all-black coloration and large, rounded head with no beak make it easy to tell apart from the killer whale.

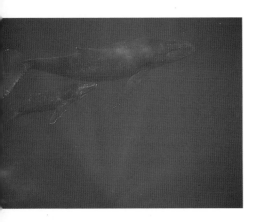

The humpback whale is bulkier in appearance than most rorquals. This mother and calf were photographed off the coast of Hawaii.

Appearance and Habits

The body of a whale is extremely well adapted to life in water, and one of the most striking features about this animal is its streamlined shape. Whales are very fast swimmers. The giant blue whale and the smaller sei whale have elongated, torpedo-shaped bodies, which enable them to swim at great speeds with little water resistance. The slower-swimming right and bowhead whales have more rotund bodies, built like tugboats, which are designed for slow swimming but quick turning and maneuvering in shallow water. The submarine-shaped sperm and pilot whales are built for quick, deep diving and rapid surfacing. The lively dolphins show excellent streamlining, many of them having slim bodies with elongated snouts. Porpoises, by comparison, are more rounded, and as a result, are not such fast swimmers.

The skin of a whale is smooth, lacking external structures like hairs that would impede movement through the water, and the whale is able to make minute adjustments to the surface shape and texture of the skin to minimize drag.

The whale's tail lies horizontally in the water, and not vertically, as in fish. The tail stock, by which it is attached to the body, is a powerful, muscular part that provides the power for the whale to swim. Forward movement mostly comes from the upstroke of the tail, the downstroke being a much more relaxed movement. Steering and balance are maintained by the flippers and by body movements. When a whale begins a dive, its head is pushed down; then with a powerful stroke of the tail the body starts to follow it.

In some species, most notably the humpback, the back is arched prominently and the tail comes up out of the water. As the body continues to slip below the water, the tail gives a further upstroke, leaving an circular, oily-looking swirl on the surface called the fluke print. The old whalers once thought this was a patch of oil excreted by the whale, but it is really just a disturbance caused by the movements of the powerful tail.

A number of species of whale indulge in a spectacular form of behavior known as breaching, when the whale leaps out of the water and falls back with a huge splash. This is a thrilling spectacle for whale watchers, but cannot be predicted. Young humpback whales regularly engage in breaching, sometimes completely leaving the water, but several other species have also been observed breaching, including right whales, killers, and even sperm whales.

The spinner dolphin, found in large schools in tropical waters, leaps completely clear of the water, spinning its body as it does so. When a school of over a hundred of these attractive dolphins do this together in a sparkling tropical sea, the effect is breathtaking. Leaping clear of the water is an effort for a dolphin, but for a huge humpback whale, weighing many tons, it must require a huge expenditure of energy. It has been estimated that only two or three powerful beats of the tail are required to get the whale out of the water. Sometimes a breach happens just once, but occasionally an individual whale will breach repeatedly, providing any whale watchers in the area with a never-to-be-forgotten experience.

Baleen Whales

Baleen is a structure that evolved to help the whales filter seawater in order to trap their food. It is derived from a material similar to our fingernails and forms a comblike curtain in the mouth of the whale. To accommodate the baleen plates, the baleen whales all have large heads and mouths.

In order to feed, they swim along with the mouth open and take in a huge volume of seawater. The mouth then partially closes and the tongue is pushed up, forcing the seawater back out of the mouth through the baleen plates. Any organisms present in the seawater are trapped in the mouth and can then be swallowed.

Some species of baleen whale, such as the right whales, have very fine baleen, enabling them to feed on small organisms like microscopic plants and animals. Others, like the blue whale, for example, have slightly coarser baleen, which allows them to trap krill, an abundant species of shrimp measuring just 1 centimeter (.4 inch) or so in length. A number of baleen whales, such as the minke and humpback, are primarily fish eaters, so their baleen is stronger and shorter than that of the plankton feeders. The gray whale feeds mainly on mollusks and crustaceans dredged out of the mud in shallow seas, and it has the coarsest baleen of all.

The right whales were once hunted continuously by the old whalers. Because they move slowly, tend to live near the shore, and float when dead, these whales were considered the ideal quarry—hence, their common name. The right whales were principally hunted for their enormously long baleen, but they also yielded a rich supply of oil. The huge mouth of the right whale is one of

Humpback whales in the deep waters off Point Adolphus, Alaska, show their arched backs, the first sign that they are preparing to dive. This area is a favorite feeding ground for humpbacks in summer, as it provides a rich supply of fish.

A bottle-nosed dolphin breaks the surface momentarily to breathe through its open blowhole. Its sleek, streamlined body is designed for speed.

its most distinctive features; it would be possible for a dozen people to stand inside it! The black right whale is sometimes separated into two species: the north Atlantic and south Atlantic. They live at opposite ends of the Atlantic Ocean and are unlikely to ever meet, so they should at least be considered as separate races. The north Atlantic right whale is a very rare animal. This whale enjoys a fully protected status, as there are only a few hundred left in the world.

The Greenland right whale, or bowhead whale, has the longest baleen of any whale and was hunted relentlessly for this valuable product. It has approximately three hundred baleen plates on either side of its mouth, with the longest measuring over 8.2 feet (2.5 meters). As with other right whales, it also yields huge volumes of oil. Sadly, this very rare species is still hunted by the Eskimo today.

The gray whale is an odd-looking whale with a blotched skin and heavy encrustations of barnacles and whale lice. Found in the northern Pacific Ocean, gray whales are best seen along the coasts of California and Mexico, especially during migration and at their breeding lagoons off Baja California. The gray whale earned the name "devil fish" in the nineteenth century because of the violent way in which it would defend itself and its offspring from the attacks of whalers. Anyone who is fortunate enough to watch gray whales in the wild today will agree that this is a most unsuitable name. Gray whales are peaceable animals that lead quiet lives in the warm, shallow lagoons off the Mexican coast. If aware of a small boat near them they will often approach it closely, raising their heads high out of the water to get a better look at the occupants. Although capable of capsizing a small dinghy with one flick of the tail, these whales will slip quietly back into the water with hardly a ripple. They can hardly be blamed for defending themselves if attacked with harpoons.

The rorquals, or "pleated" whales, are large, streamlined, fast-swimming whales of the open sea. Their bodies are designed for swimming quickly over great distances. Each rorqual has pointed flippers, a pointed head, a pleated throat, and a dorsal fin near the tail. At one time it was thought that the pleated throat was a type of streamlining and an aid to fast swimming, but now it is known that it enables the throat to expand when taking in seawater.

A distinctively marked tail of a humpback whale about to dive in very deep water close to the Alaskan shore. The whale may stay under for several minutes in search of food before returning to the surface to breathe.

Common dolphins sometimes live in schools numbering hundreds, and when they all come to the surface together the water turns white with spray.

Rorquals range in size from the 100-foot- (30.3-meter-) long blue whale, to the 35-foot- (10.6-meter-) long minke. The humpback whale is similar in some respects, having the pleated throat, but it is not as streamlined as the rorquals and has much longer flippers and a rough skin with barnacles attached in places. The rorquals are very businesslike in their habits, concentrating on feeding, while the humpback is more playful, and is more likely to be seen rolling at the surface or breaching.

The whaling nations systematically worked their way through the populations of these splendid animals, reducing their numbers to critical levels and bringing some of them to the verge of extinction. A full-grown blue whale was a real prize to a whaling vessel, with all the crew taking a share of the profits, so there was every incentive to kill as many as possible. After the blue whales had been reduced from a population of hundreds of thousands to just a few thousand, the whaling fleets turned to the fin whale, a slightly smaller species reaching a length of about 82.5 feet (25 meters) at the most. These also suffered a decline and are now harder to find. The sei and tropical (Bryde's) whales were next to be hunted, although both of these are more difficult to find due to the way in which they disperse over wide areas of the oceans. Seis reach a length of 59 feet (17.8 meters), while tropical whales usually do not exceed 49 feet (14.8 meters).

The smallest baleen whale is the minke, and this is now the main target of the whalers, particularly in the north Atlantic. Rarely exceeding 31 feet (9.4 meters) in length, minkes still have reasonably healthy populations in temperate waters. The minke is easily recognized by its ridged snout, noticeably recurved dorsal fin set well back near the tail, and above all, white spots on the flippers. Some individuals also have a tendency to investigate small boats and will make close approaches; this makes them an easy target for the whalers. It is suspected that with the decline in numbers of the larger species of rorqual, plankton and fish stocks actually increased. This allowed the minke whales, which were not being hunted at the time, to take advantage of the extra food and increase their own populations. This is still no excuse for hunting them, however, as there is every chance that their populations could fall to dangerously low levels as well.

Toothed Whales

The toothed whales range in size from the sperm whale, at up to 60 feet (18.2 meters) long, and other giants like the killer whale and some of the beaked whales, at around 35 feet (10.6 meters), to the smaller dolphins and porpoises, at around 6.5 feet (2 meters). Their food consists mainly of fish, squid, crustaceans, and in some cases, other marine mammals. Each species shows some special adaptation to a method of feeding or type of food. Many of the smaller species are coastal, feeding in shallow waters close to the shore. Others live in the open ocean, far from land, and little is known about them.

The mysterious beaked whales are deep divers and are rarely encountered at sea. Much of what is known about them is the result of chance encounters and studies made of beached specimens, usually found dead.

The sperm whale is the largest toothed whale—and one that has attracted the attention of humans for centuries. Everything about this whale is extraordinary. Several qualities have made this whale the stuff of legends: its great size, its immense head, its ability to dive to over 3,300 feet (1,001

Bottle-nosed dolphins are playful creatures and will often leap clear of the water. If trained in a dolphinarium, they will do this in response to a signal, or perhaps in return for a reward of food, but in the open sea they will do this at will, possibly just for fun.

meters) and stay down for over an hour, its ferocity when hunted, and its body, packed with oils and other valuable commodities. Hunting the sperm whale has always been a dangerous pursuit, and many human lives have been lost as a result, but nowhere near as many as the lives of sperm whales that have been lost. Thousands were taken every year during the peak of the whaling boom, but now, as with all the other whales, stocks are depleted and the sperm whale is harder to find.

This whale hunts its food in total darkness, far below the surface of the sea. The sperm whale finds its food by a form of echo-location. It is thought to be able to produce high-frequency sounds that are strong enough to stun prey. The giant squid is its favorite food, and the bodies of sperm whales often show circular scars along the flanks and around the head—the results of fierce battles fought between the two animals.

The Pacific white-sided dolphin has up to twenty-eight small, pointed teeth, typical of all the dolphins, in each jaw, which it uses to help it feed on squid, anchovies, and hake.

Common dolphins in the Sea of Cortez, Mexico, have sought out warmer waters of the southern winter, which takes place between July and November.

The bodies of whales and dolphins, like that of this bottle-nosed dolphin, are often covered with scars and scratches. These may be the result of encounters with predators like sharks or killer whales, or the result of fights between rivals of the same species.

The grossly enlarged, bulbous head of the sperm whale is largely made up of an oily substance called spermaceti. This material can solidify at low temperatures and it is thought to help alter the buoyancy of the whale and assist it in diving and ascending. At normal body temperatures the spermaceti is a liquid, but if its temperature drops, by coming into closer contact with cold seawater, it solidifies, increasing the density of the head and making it easier for the whale to dive.

The killer whale is an altogether more streamlined whale. It is instantly recognized by its striking black-and-white markings and, in the case of males, a 6.5-foot- (2-meter-) tall dorsal fin. Killer whales are regarded as the supreme hunters of the oceans, the equivalent of packs of wolves on land. They are found in schools varying in amounts from three to four to as many as forty individuals. Some are wide ranging, hunting their food over a vast area of the oceans. Others have a more restricted range, preferring to stay in one area, such as a large bay or the waters between groups of islands, and learning to exploit all the food available in that area.

The impressive array of teeth in the mouth of a killer whale enables it to catch and kill anything from fish and birds to large sharks and seals. It will even prey on other whales. There are well-documented accounts of packs of killer whales attacking the largest of all whales, the blue, and tearing huge chunks out of it, until it dies from exhaustion and loss of blood. Many killer whales feed on fish and actually position themselves in river mouths or near strong currents to take best advantage of the movements of large fish like salmon. The killer whales that live off Peninsula Valdez, Argentina, ride the surf onto the beach and pluck seals from their resting places on dry land, while others take seals from ice floes in Antarctica. It is not surprising, then, that this is a very successful species and one that is found throughout the world.

Most people make their first acquaintance with killer whales in captivity, as this is one species of whale that seems to adapt well to life in a dolphinarium. They are soon trained to respond to their keeper's commands and jump through hoops, perform somersaults, and even allow humans to place their heads inside their mouths! Many people consider this to be a degrading spectacle, and keeping any species of whale or dolphin captive is becoming less acceptable now.

There is much more of an interest in watching whales in the wild, and far more opportunities exist today for people to go to the whale's natural habitat and watch it behaving normally. Whale watching is an extremely profitable industry. It has done an enormous amount of good for whales by increasing the public's awareness of these animals.

The dolphins are a very large family, and some, like the common and bottle-nosed dolphins, are found almost worldwide. Most dolphins reach a length of around 6.5 feet (2 meters), and they are very streamlined and elegant animals. They are designed for speed and life in the open sea. Many delight sailors by bow-riding ahead of a boat, a habit they

acquired by swimming in front of large whales. Some dolphins live together in schools of hundreds, but others are more solitary. Tens of thousands are killed every year, and populations of a number of species are critically low. Tuna fisheries are responsible for large numbers of dolphin deaths, as they are easily entangled in the nets set for tuna, but many thousands are killed deliberately by fishermen who see them as competitors for the same dwindling fish stocks. They are still hunted for food in some seas, but this practice is in decline.

As one whale dives after breathing, its blow disperses in the cold air of an Alaskan morning, but it is quickly joined by the blow of a second whale swimming alongside it.

Long-Distance Migrants

Tropical seas may look blue, warm, and inviting to us, but to a plankton-feeding whale they are a biological desert, lacking in plankton and other suitable forms of food. The very blue color, reflect-

ing a sunny tropical sky, is an indicator of the clarity of the water; the clearer the water, the less plankton there is suspended in it. The most productive waters are mainly found in the colder parts of the world. Ocean currents carry dissolved nutrients toward the poles, where upwellings then bring them to the surface. This stimulates a massive growth of microscopic plants, which in turn supports microscopic animals and starts off a highly productive food chain.

These are important feeding areas for the majority of the great baleen whales, which spend as much time as possible there. Unfortunately, during the polar winter the seas often freeze over, light levels are diminished, and plant plankton growth ceases. The whales find little or no food, so they leave for warmer waters. These waters enable them to maintain their high body temperatures, even if they have to stop feeding. This necessitates making long migrations from the polar oceans to the warmer waters of the tropics.

Gray whales feed around the shores of Alaska and then migrate all the way down the West Coast of North America to the sheltered waters of the coast of Mexico and the Sea of Cortez. There they give birth during the northern winter. Humpback whales, which feed off Newfoundland in summer, swim down the East Coast of North America to reach Bermuda in winter, some carrying on as far as the West Indies and the coast of Venezuela, only to return north again the following spring. The

Gray whales travel to warm waters to breed, but find their food in colder waters farther north. They favor shallow lagoons from where they can scoop mud from the bottom and filter their food, usually shrimp, worms, and shellfish.

warmer waters are more suitable for the birth of the young whales, which at first lack the protective layer of blubber that insulates adult whales from cold water. If young whales were born in polar waters, they would have great difficulty in keeping up their body temperatures.

As soon as they are born they start to suckle and put on body fat at a rapid rate. During this time in the warmer waters the adult whales do not feed, but live instead on their stored fat. The stresses of fasting, giving birth, and suckling a calf are too much for some whales, and a number die at this time. Most of the large whales mate at this time as well, so by the time the females are ready to return to their cold but productive feeding areas, they are likely to be pregnant and accompanied by a calf.

On returning to the feeding grounds, the females quickly restore their body weight and the young whales continue to grow, feeding partly on milk, but also learning to feed using their baleen.

During the course of a long life, perhaps as much as fifty years, a great whale may cover many thousands of miles in its annual two-way journeys from feeding to breeding grounds.

At one time the great whales were found in huge numbers in these cold but food-rich polar regions, but once the modern whaling fleets discovered their whereabouts and learned to hunt them with powerful harpoons, the numbers rapidly declined, bringing some species almost to the point of extinction. After many years of limited protection and reduced whaling quotas, some species are beginning to make a slight recovery, but the remaining numbers are only a fraction of the populations that existed before mechanized commercial whaling began in earnest. The blue whale is one of the species that was hunted relentlessly until the population reached dangerously low levels. Its numbers are still critically low.

The striking, streamlined black-and-white head of the killer whale makes it easy to identify; pilot whales and melon-headed whales have all-black heads.

SEA MAMMALS

Its fierce disposition, the theme of so many traveller's tales, must be subject to moods, for Nansen tells of walruses so gentle that he had to strike them on the snout with his stick before they would move. Doubtless Nansen's walruses had not yet benefitted by the educating influence of contact with man.

—F.G. Aflalo, *A Sketch Of The Natural History Of The British Islands*, 1897

Walruses

The walrus is a massive, seal-like mammal with a bristling moustache and a pair of long tusks. The enormous, hairless body, usually reddish in color, which looks so ungainly on land, is graceful and surprisingly fast moving in water. With their peculiar expressions, tiny, sunken eyes, wrinkled skin, and bulbous noses, walruses appear so comical that it is hard to imagine that they are superbly well adapted to life in the Arctic seas.

This is a very gregarious and highly social animal, almost always found in large concentrations. Walruses generally cluster together on ice floes or stony shores. As the polar ice advances and retreats, they migrate together in large herds, and only very rarely does one become lost and find itself farther south, perhaps reaching the shores of northern Britain.

Raking the seabed with their 3.3-foot- (1-meter-) long tusks, walruses unearth cockles, clams, and other buried mollusks. Using sensory bristles, they locate these creatures as they emerge from the mud. To a lesser extent, walruses also feed on fish and sometimes even smaller species of seals. Occasionally a tusk becomes damaged, perhaps through hitting a buried rock, but this does not prevent walruses from feeding, and individuals are frequently seen in an apparently healthy state with one tusk much shorter than the other.

The huge tusks of the walrus, sometimes reaching 3.3 feet (1 meter) in length, are used to gouge through the mud on the seabed and dig out clams. At first juveniles have short tusks, but following weaning, they soon develop.

Following page:

When space is at a premium on a popular hauling-out beach, walruses must squeeze in on top of each other and try to avoid damage from neighbors' tusks, but these sociable animals seem to enjoy a crush.

If a walrus hits a tusk on a rocky seabed, it can easily cause damage, but as long as at least one is in good condition, the animal is able to feed. Walruses are still hunted in some remote places for their tusks, oil, and skins, but for the most part they are protected. There may be as many as 150,000 left in the Arctic.

Walruses are born in April and May, and the females may then mate again. The pups are suckled by their mothers for about one year, during which time their weight will increase from 88 to 352 pounds (40 to 158 kilograms). Gestation and suckling both last for about one year, and most females breed in every third or fourth year. Walruses are still hunted in some parts of the Arctic; they yield oil, skins, and ivory. Although the level of hunting now is less than it was earlier this century, this is still not a common animal and in some parts of its range the populations are low enough for it to be locally endangered. There may be around 150,000 walruses scattered around the Arctic at present.

Sirenians

The sirenians, or sea cows, are also large, water-dwelling mammals. Members of the order Sirenia, they include the dugone and manatee, which are distantly related to elephants and look rather like grossly overweight and lethargic dolphins. Unlike the seals and walruses they are completely

A pair of walruses engages in a half-hearted battle. Usually these squabbles end amicably, but sometimes severe damage can be done by the tusk ripping through the skin and blubber of a rival.

There may not always be a beach nearby, so a passing ice floe will make a temporary resting place for a group of walruses. A juvenile with short tusks rests among the adults.

A large, flat-topped ice floe is a safe and convenient stopover for several small groups of walruses. They can easily slip off into the water when they need to feed on the seabed below, and on their drifting island they are safe from disturbance from the land.

Round Island, Alaska, is a favorite hauling-out site for walruses, highly sociable animals who always enjoy each other's company. Hundreds can be counted at times, entirely covering beaches.

aquatic, being unable to haul themselves out of the water and rest on land. They may just be able to lift their heads out of the water to reach a particularly tempting plant, but they cannot move around on land like a seal. They inhabit warm, shallow seas and are fond of estuaries and sluggish rivers, where they can find sea grasses and other succulent aquatic vegetation to feed on. They have virtually no body hair, apart from around the mouth, and are covered with a loose, leathery skin. The head of a manatee is large, merging into the bulky body without any sign of a neck.

Sirenians are reported to suckle their young by resting upright in the water and supporting the pup gently with one flipper; this tender scene is thought to be the origin of the mermaid legend.

An adult sirenian reaches a length of around 13 feet (3.9 meters) and weigh up to 1,100 pounds (495 kilograms). The sexes are similar and hard to distinguish in the water, unless a female is seen suckling a calf. They live mostly solitary lives, browsing quietly on vegetation on aquatic plants and occasionally reaching up to take plants from overhanging banks. Sirenians are shy of humans and easily disturbed by boats, so they usually avoid harbors and busy rivers. They are vulnerable to pollution and industrial contaminants and are easily injured by speeding motor boats, so they are becoming increasingly restricted to a few sheltered localities. The Florida race of manatee, found around the waters of Everglades National Park, has some degree of protection, but the Caribbean race, although more numerous, is still hunted for its palatable meat and is declining.

Seals

Seals are earless and placed in a separate family from the sea lions and fur seals, which do possess small ear flaps. Seals have streamlined bodies and paddlelike flippers, which cannot be turned forward or used very effectively for movement on land or ice. When on land they crawl or undulate their fat bodies, looking

Manatees are known to move into freshwater, especially during winter. During this season, they are attracted to warm, freshwater springs that offer a promise of food.

Adult manatees consume water plants, but the young are fed on mothers' milk. A full-grown adult can measure 13 feet (3.9 meters) in length and weigh 1,100 pounds (495 kilograms).

This 13-foot- (3.9-meter-) long manatee is actually a gentle giant. Shy of humans, it usually swims off at the sound of a boat. A few have learned to trust swimmers and may allow themselves to be touched.

A large group of female southern elephant seals is hauled out on a beach on King George Island, Antarctica, during its annual molt. The ragged appearance of the pelts will improve once the old fur has fallen out.

like gigantic slugs or caterpillars. Despite the apparent difficulties in moving out of the water, some species do travel considerable distances, often along well-worn trails, to safe hauling-out sites or sheltered places where the young are born. Seals come into their own in the water, however, when they use their streamlined, muscular bodies to great advantage in swimming after prey or escaping from predators.

One of the smallest seals is the harbor, or common, seal. It is found close to shore around the Arctic and the northern shores of North America, Britain, Europe, and Japan. This seal is shy of humans, probably as a result of centuries of relentless persecution. It sometimes uses beaches, but prefers to haul out on isolated rocks and islands, always remaining close enough to the water to be able to plunge back at the first sign of danger.

Pups are born in spring or early summer and are able to swim alongside their mothers within hours of birth. They are fed on a rich milk for about five weeks, during which time they triple their birth weight. After this very short period of dependence on their mothers, the young are then able to fend for themselves.

The gray seal is much larger, sometimes reaching a length of 10 feet (3.1 meters) and a weight of

The southern, or Kerguelen, fur seal is found on the South Shetland Islands. Reaching lengths of up to 6.5 feet (2 meters), these are among the smaller sea lions and are making a good recovery after many years of persecution for their pelts. Hardly seen at all in the 1920s, this seal is now found in colonies of thousands.

616 pounds (277 kilograms), and this species prefers rocky, exposed situations on the remote coastal areas. Most of the world's population lives around the shores of Britain, but the gray seal is also seen off the shores of Norway and Iceland and across the Atlantic around the Gulf of St. Lawrence and Newfoundland. This is a deep-diving seal, going down to depths of at least 330 feet (100 meters) in search of large fish. The bull gray seal can be recognized by its "Roman" nose and great bulk. It may bear scars from battles with other bulls during the mating season.

Bearded seals are also very large seals with the ability to make deep dives. The extra long whiskers are highly sensitive and help the seal locate its food, mostly mollusks and crustaceans, on the seabed.

Antarctica is home to three other species of seal, which are able to cope with this permanently cold world and exploit its rich supplies of food. The most abundant seal, indeed one of the most abundant mammals in the world, is the crabeater seal, with an estimated world population of over fifty million animals. This attractive seal, which actually eats krill rather than crab, has a silvery coat and measures up to 10 feet (3.1 meters) in length. It is confined to the ever-shifting pack ice. Unlike other seals, it does not form large colonies, but lives in scattered groups of twos and threes spread out over a vast area. This seal's main enemy is the killer whale, which hunts it among the ice floes; many adult crabeaters bear the scars of close encounters with this large predator. Although the crabeaters are so numerous, they have never been exploited by human hunters, due mainly to the remoteness and difficult nature of the habitat in which they live.

Harbor seals swim well, catching fish in shallow waters near the coast. Young harbor seals are able to swim alongside their mothers only a few hours after they are born. During courtship, males become very energetic, sometimes leaping out of the water like dolphins.

Leopard seals are far less numerous, but the population still numbers around 500,000. They are noted for their ferocity—or at least their alleged ferocity. They prey on penguins, large fish, and the young of other seals. Leopard seals have a natural cunning, which enables them to cooperate and collectively terrorize penguin colonies during the breeding season. In such situations, two seals will position themselves near the colony and catch penguins as they return from fishing trips. With a deft flick of the head, the seal can kill and skin a penguin in a few seconds.

These seals have a natural curiosity and will investigate small boats that appear in their territory by suddenly surfacing alongside. They are easily scared off by shouting or banging on the sides of the boat, but some Antarctic explorers treat them as dangerous animals and shoot them on sight. Although they can slither over ice faster than a human can run, and they will definitely make for anyone they see between them and their route to the sea, there are no reliable records of unprovoked attacks on humans.

Weddell seals are commonly found on the coastal Antarctic ice. Though they are rarely seen far from land, these seals sometimes stray to the extreme southern shores of New Zealand, Tasmania, and South America. Weddell seals are deep divers and are also able to stay down for long periods. They have been detected at depths of over 1,980 feet (600 meters) and regularly make dives lasting

A pair of southern elephant seals argues at a colony on the Falkland Islands in the south Atlantic. Most arguments end in one of the seals retreating with no harm being done. Only bulls fight hard enough to draw blood and do real damage to each other.

Most of the world's population of gray seals lives off the rocky western and northern shores of Great Britain, preferring isolated rocks and islands in wild places. They can dive to depths of 330 feet (100 meters), staying under for as long as twenty minutes while they chase fish, squid, and other creatures of the seabed such as lobsters.

The long whiskers of the bearded seal help it locate its prey on the seabed at depths of down to 330 feet (100 meters). In the murky waters of the Arctic Ocean and Bering Sea, food is plentiful and its diet of thick-shelled clams and crabs wears down its teeth.

A young bull southern elephant seal rests on a Falkland Islands beach. Much of the seal's life is spent at sea, but it does spend some time on shore during the breeding season. When it matures, this animal may weigh in at 4.4 tons (3.9 metric tons) and measure up to 21.5 feet (6.5 meters) in length, making it the world's largest seal.

The bull northern elephant seal can inflate its strange proboscis to make its head look larger and more frightening. At breeding colonies, the large bulls defend their harems of females to prevent other bulls from stealing them.

The most heavily hunted of the world's seals, the harp seal is valued for its coat. Fortunately, many harp seals live on remote pack ice, thus avoiding hunters entirely.

The crabeater seal lives in the remotest regions of Antarctica, remaining among the shifting pack ice, where it is difficult to observe. Its main enemy is the killer whale, and many bear the scars of close encounters with this fierce predator. Despite this it is thought to be the most abundant seal in the world, with a population of many millions.

over an hour. From the surface it is sometimes possible to hear the twittering, birdlike calls they use to locate fish in the dark. Unlike the supposedly aggressive leopard seal, Weddell seals have the reputation of being the friendly seals of the Antarctic, allowing humans to approach them closely as they bask in the sun. In winter they stay in the water permanently, coming to the surface to breathe through holes in the ice. They keep the ice holes open by gnawing at the edges with their teeth. Weddell seals also use their teeth to make steps in the ice to help when they haul out to bask. As might be expected, the older adults often have worn and chipped teeth.

Pups are born on the ice in September and October, and at first have a pale gray, downy coat. After three to four weeks they lose this and grow a darker, juvenile coat and are then ready to enter the water. Both courtship and mating take place in the water soon after the pups are born, and then the adults disperse to their feeding grounds. This seal is difficult to census because of its numerous small, scattered colonies, but there may be up to 400,000 living around the Antarctic.

The elephant seals are the real giants of the seal world. With adult males reaching a length of 21.5 feet (6.5 meters), there are no other sea mammals to rival them apart from the great whales. Elephant seals are found on the West Coast of the United States from California to Alaska, as well as on the Atlantic coast of Argentina, on various Antarctic islands, and at scattered localities around New Zealand, Australia, and South Africa. The elephant seals are divided into two species, the northern elephant seal and the southern elephant seal. The northern species is the rarest, numbering only about thirty thousand individuals. This is a remarkable recovery from the estimated twenty animals that survived the ruthless hunting of the nineteenth century.

Most of the northern population is found on islands off Baja California and southern California. The southern elephant seal is much more abundant, and the world population is thought to number at least 600,000 animals. They, too, were hunted in the nineteenth century, but the remoteness of many of their colonies allowed enough to survive to provide the nucleus of a successful breeding stock. As a fully protected species, the elephant seal is now threatened only by overfishing and pollution.

The southern elephant seals spend much of the winter at sea, often at considerable distances from land. They feed on fish and squid caught by diving in deep water. In spring some haul out on ice floes, but most prefer beaches. Mature males are the first to arrive, and they lay claim to beach areas with aggressive displays. In such a display, the animal inflates its bulbous nose, or trunk. This increases the apparent size of the head and helps to intensify the loudness and resonance of the animal's roar. If one male approaches another's territory too closely, a fierce battle will ensue and one will have to give in and move away. These battles often leave both victor and vanquished bearing deep scars.

After the males have established territories, the pregnant females arrive. The males organize the females into groups, and the young are born about a week later. The pups are fed on a rich milk, which enables them to triple their weight in only three weeks. The 3.3-foot-long (1-meter-long) pups grow rapidly and are weaned within a few weeks. During this time, their mothers mate and are soon ready to return to the sea once more. Together with the males, the pups, which by now have developed sleek coats, also start to leave the beaches, and quite soon the scene of all this

Ice floes in Glacier Bay, Alaska, are often utilized by harbor seals. This small species is a fish eater, a habit that leads it into conflict with fishermen, who see it as a threat. The sad result is that many are shot each year.

Following page:

Weddell seals inhabit the coastal ice floes of Antarctica, rarely being seen far from the shore. They enjoy basking in the sun and sleep soundly in the open for long periods. In winter they remain in the water all the time, keeping a breathing hole open in the ice by gnawing at the sides with their teeth, which usually appear chipped and worn.

A leopard seal resting on an ice floe looks fierce and aggressive, but it can be rather timid if approached by humans. Its curiosity leads to it approaching small boats to investigate the occupants, but its real prey is penguins, large fish, and the occasional pup of other species of seal.

The harbor, or common, seal is a small mammal of coastal waters, preferring estuaries, sea lochs, and large natural harbors. Rather nervous of man on account of centuries of persecution, it can usually be found hauled out in small groups on isolated rocks and sandbanks, always close enough to the water to plunge in at the slightest sign of trouble.

frenzied activity is quite deserted.

Midsummer is the time when food reserves are replenished, as the seals feed ravenously after their enforced fast on the beach. By the end of summer they are ready to return to the beach once more, but this time in order to molt out of their worn coats. They spend up to one month on the beach, crammed together in smelly wallows, grunting and squabbling with each other as they shed strips of the old fur and grow the new fur beneath. Then they return to the sea once more to fatten up during the winter. By the age of about ten years, a male is strong enough to hold its own territory; a female is able to breed from the third or fourth year.

Fur seals are thought to have first appeared in the colder regions of the northern Pacific Ocean, where one species is still found. It is likely that they spread southward along the eastern Pacific, where there are some cold currents that reach areas like the Galapagos Islands and various sub-Antarctic islands. Fur seals are mostly smaller than sea lions and have more prominently pointed noses, pronounced ear tufts, and a thick, velvety underfur.

The northern fur seal is the most well known of all the fur seal species and has some well-established colonies on the Pribilof Islands, off the coast of Alaska. This species is still hunted, but stocks are carefully watched and quotas are set, so the population is managing to increase and is no longer thought to be at a dangerously low level. Fur seals feed in quite deep water, regularly making dives of 330 feet (100 meters) or more to take fish and squid.

In midsummer they return to their breeding islands, where dominant males round up harems of around forty pregnant females. The pups, looking like Labrador retriever puppies and sounding rather like them as well, are born after a few weeks and suckled by their mothers for about one week. After this they are gathered together and left for days on end as the females go off to sea to feed. When a female returns, she is able to locate her own young from among the throng and single it out for a feed.

The pups do not grow as rapidly as the young of some other species, as they are fed so sporadically. They spend up to three months on the breeding beach, playing together and sometimes venturing into the sea, before finally leaving the beach and joining the newly molted adults for a migration southward to escape the approaching northern winter.

Other species of fur seal have a similar lifestyle, living in colonies during the breeding season and then dispersing over their feeding grounds during the winter. Most populations were brought to the verge of extinction by nineteenth-century hunters, but enough survived to allow a recovery.

The Galapagos fur seal is unusual in that it lives on the equator. During the heat of the day, these seals haul out onto rocks with overhangs and lie in the shade until temperatures fall. During El Niño years, when the cold Antarctic current fails to sweep past the islands, their breeding success is reduced and they do not rear many young.

The Pribilof Islands off the coast of Alaska are home to large colonies of the northern fur seal, now repopulating that area as a result of protection from hunters. The long whiskers help the fur seal locate its prey, usually fish and squid, in dark waters at depths of about 330 feet (100 meters). Fur seals have more pointed noses than sea lions and a thick, velvetlike underfur.

Point Adolphus, Alaska, is a well-known site for Steller's sea lions, which are often seen resting on rocks close to the shore. The deep waters of Glacier Bay offer good fishing; plentiful supplies of fish and squid have helped this species maintain a high population here, although it is most abundant in the chilly and windswept Aleutian Islands.

Sea Lions

Like their close relatives, the fur seals, the sea lions are thought to have first appeared in the northern Pacific Ocean. Thereafter, they spread out to colonize other areas in the Southern Hemisphere. Sea lions rarely venture as far north as the Arctic and so far have not been seen in the north Atlantic Ocean. Sea lions have a coarse fur that lacks silky underfur. They are fairly agile on land, using their flippers like limbs for climbing and walking.

Sea lions often occur in the same places as the fur seals, such as on the Galapagos Islands, for example, but they prefer to haul out on open beaches away from heavy surf. Unlike the fur seals, which seek shade in hot, sunny weather, they appear to enjoy basking in the sunshine for short periods. Breeding usually takes place later in the season, and they tend not to move so far offshore when feeding. The California sea lion is the species most likely to be seen as a performing animal in a circus, usually incorrectly called a "seal."

Various populations of sea lions are found around the Pacific Ocean, with the California sea lion being the most frequently encountered and the best-known species. The Galapagos sea lion is considered to be a subspecies of the California. More than any other, this is the animal that greets visi-

A bull California sea lion roars at any other bull who approaches his territory. From mid-May onward they defend territories vigorously, but throughout the year they are very vocal. Females squabble as well, and the pups start to squeal for their mothers soon after they are born, so the sea lion colony is an especially noisy place.

tors to the Galapagos as they step ashore from a boat on any beach on the islands. Colonies are noisy and lively at any time, but during the breeding season, which starts in May on the California and Mexican coasts, the din increases. Large bulls gather their harems of females together, usually managing to keep about twelve to themselves. The bulls roar and bellow at each other, and the cows keep up a constant bickering.

The pups are born into this noisy atmosphere in June and add to the general cacophony by making their own wailing cries. Mothers are able to identify their young by their individual voices. About two weeks after giving birth, the mothers mate again. Thereafter, the bulls gradually lose interest in them. At this point, the males disperse at sea and restore their energies by a spell of feeding. When they eventually decide to haul out on a beach, they gather together in a "bachelor" colony, isolated from the breeding colonies where the females are looking after their young. The females, meanwhile, suckle their young for several weeks, and from time to time take them on short trips to sea. Some pups remain with their mothers for up to a year, leaving them just before the start of the next breeding season.

In common with many of the other seals, fur seals, and sea lions, they live mostly on a diet of fish

After feeding at sea, a Galapagos sea lion returns to the beach to rest. The claws on the hind flippers are useful for scratching and grooming the fur as it dries out in the hot, equatorial sun.

A female Hooker's sea lion and her pup on Enderbury Island, New Zealand, are in a safe resting place in the middle of the breeding colony. The pups are born in December, during the southern summer, and after a few weeks will be left on the beach by their mothers, who go off to sea to find fish. The mothers return to suckle their pups every few days.

Disturbed by a boat approaching too closely, a group of Steller's sea lions plunges into the sea from its favorite hauling-out rock in Glacier Bay, Alaska. They are still hunted in some areas and, as a result, are very nervous when they sense danger.

and squid. The Galapagos population may number twenty thousand animals. The California population may be as high as fifty thousand individuals.

Stretching in a long arc from Alaska toward Siberia, the Aleutian Islands are wild, remote, and windswept, but they evidently provide the perfect conditions for the Steller's sea lion, which is found there in great numbers; as many as 300,000 have been estimated, and this may only be one third of the total world population. They feed on fish and squid, sometimes competing with human fishermen for the same species, and in a few areas, they are hunted for oil and skins.

At the other end of the world, off the remote islands south of New Zealand, there are increasing numbers of the rare Hooker's sea lion. This species was ruthlessly hunted in the nineteenth century, mainly for skin and its rich oil, but now populations are recovering, and there may be about fifty thousand in total, with a thriving colony in the Auckland Islands.

California sea lions are streamlined and agile swimmers, easily able to chase fish among rocks or through kelp beds. They are quick to investigate human swimmers in the water and easily outmaneuver them.

SHARKS

[The Greenland shark] is a great foe to the whale, which it bites and annoys while living, and devours when dead. Insensible to pain and tenacious of life, as are all the larger sharks, this species is pre-eminently so.

—Frank Buckland, *The Natural History of British Fishes*, 1880

Sharks have always aroused mixed emotions. Fear, curiosity, and a grudging respect for their great strength and ruthless hunting skills have always been associated with shark sightings. For centuries they been thought of as fearless killers and a danger to humans. The very sight of the pointed snout, the large mouth, the cold, unblinking eyes, the triangular fins, and the sinuous body is enough to cause panic among swimmers.

There are around three hundred species of shark known to science, but of those only twenty-seven species are known to have made attacks on people or their boats. Shark attacks receive plenty of publicity, but the statistics show that there is very little likelihood of any swimmer being attacked unless in very close proximity to a dangerous species, and even then it may not be inclined to make an attack. In cold waters, sharks never attack.

One thing that can be said about sharks with some certainty is that they are unpredictable. A potentially dangerous species like the great white shark may swim among human divers and completely ignore them. Or it may come out of nowhere and launch a savage attack. Even though only a relatively small number of shark species is dangerous to humans, almost any species encountered is treated as a threat, and there are many sailors and fishermen who savagely butcher any shark they might catch without first ascertaining whether or not it is harmless.

Sharks are primitive fish with a skeleton composed of cartilage, rather than the bone of the true fish. They lack the disklike scales on their bodies that true fish possess, having a covering of rough, backward-pointing, toothlike scales instead. A shark's skin is so rough that when dried it can be used as a form of sandpaper. The tough skin of the Greenland shark is used

**The gaping mouth of the great white shark shows
the fearsome array of teeth that it uses to tear
chunks of flesh from its prey. It readily attacks any
marine mammal or large fish, and human divers need
to take great care if great whites are in the vicinity.**

A blue shark swims among a shoal of mackerel, one of its favorite prey species. The mackerel scatter in a panic as the shark approaches.

A diver demonstrates the effectiveness of the Neptunic shark suit, designed to protect people from the teeth and jaws of potentially dangerous species like this blue shark. A shark is unlikely to attack like this without extreme provocation.

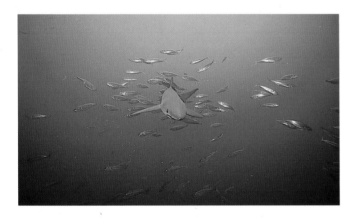

A blue shark seizes a mackerel in its jaws. Many such fish are needed to satisfy the appetite of this voracious fish, which may grow to a length of over 13 feet (3.9 meters).

The blue shark is effectively camouflaged in the open ocean. Its dark blue coloration, with the lighter blue sides and white belly, is unique to this species.

The scalloped hammerhead is a common species around the coasts of Australia. This species can be differentiated from the great hammerhead by the convex, wavy margin of its head lobes.

The oceanic whitetip shark shows many features typical of the sharks. Its extended upper tail lobe provides forward movement and lift when moved from side to side in the water. The torpedo-shaped body is designed for speed, and the mouth is set beneath the head to accentuate the streamlining. This species may attain a length of 11.5 feet (3.5 meters).

to make a form of leather for bookbinding. True fish have their gills protected behind bony gill flaps, but the sharks have five gill slits instead.

A shark's teeth are one of its most important features. In most species the teeth are triangular and have either a smooth or a serrated edge. The bite of a shark is one of its most distinctive features, and victims of shark attacks are often able to provide evidence of which species attacked them by the tooth marks left behind on their skin.

If a shark's front teeth are lost, others are ready in the row behind to replace them. The teeth do not grow in bony sockets like human teeth, but are rooted in the softer tissues of the mouth. The shark's mouth is almost always on the underside of its head, set back slightly from the tip of the snout. It is still thought by some that sharks must always roll on their sides in order to feed, but this is not the case. Observations by divers and studies of captive sharks in aquaria show that they can perfectly easily take food swimming in front of them without rolling over. If necessary, when approaching prey at the surface, for example, a shark may sometimes roll over to avoid breaking the surface, and this behavior, observed by fishermen, may be the explanation for the myth.

The capacious mouth of some of the larger sharks enables them to swallow an extraordinary variety of objects: car license plates, bottles, pieces of ship's tackle, human clothing, and a great range of animals not associated with the ocean, such as reindeer and domestic cats. All of these and many more gruesome remains, such as parts of human anatomy, have been found inside the stomachs of dead sharks. Most of the time, however, they confine their feeding to the prey species to which they are most suited. Most sharks are fish eaters, but will take other food if it is possible to catch it.

There are plenty of observations of sharks feeding on marine mammals, seabirds, turtles, and other sea creatures. The stomach and intestines of sharks are quite distinctive, being fairly short when compared with similarly sized bony fishes. The U-shaped stomach is connected to the small intestine, which has an internal spiral fold of tissue that effectively increases its surface area, thus helping the shark absorb its food.

The senses of sharks are designed to help them locate their food in the sea. Their eyes enable them to see movements and make out the shapes of objects in dim lighting. A few species are known to have color vision, but the effectiveness of this is not yet fully understood. They can see some movement in quite dim light and generally have their eyes focused in such a way that they can see distant objects clearly, thus enabling them to get an early warning of approaching prey or danger. In order to make the most of dim light levels, there is a silvery reflective layer of tissue behind the retina called the tapetum lucidum. This reflects the light passing through the retina and also accounts for the peculiar reddish glow given off by the eyes when a light is shone on them. Photographers who use flash photography to take shark pictures often end up with red-eyed sharks.

The most important sense a shark possesses is small. In most species the nostrils open on the underside of the head, and these lead to special scent-detecting organs positioned just inside them. The scent detectors are linked to the olfactory lobes of the brain, which are especially well developed in sharks. Experiments have shown that most species of sharks can accurately locate the position of prey by scent alone, being able to detect tiny quantities of blood or body fluid suspended in the water. They will swim toward an interesting scent in decreasing circles until finally homing in on it, often using the eyes at the last moment to make a precise attack. If the nostrils are plugged,

The white shark, sometimes known as the white pointer shark, is a large and ferocious species, sometimes reaching a length of 23 feet (6.9 meters). There are records of specimens of up 35 feet (10.6 meters) long. White sharks are very fast swimmers, easily overtaking dolphins and able to escape power boats. They feed on large prey, such as dolphins and turtles, and have been known to attack human divers.

this method of prey location seems not to work at all. The nostrils are spaced on either side of the head, and by turning the head from side to side as it swims the shark can judge from which direction the scent is coming most strongly and then swim toward it.

Most sharks have a very well developed lateral line, which is really a set of pressure detectors running the length of the body, giving them the ability to detect vibrations and subtle changes in water pressure. Thus, they are also able to detect prey by its movement. For example, if a fish is swimming in an odd way, perhaps because it is sick or injured, it will make

Following page:

Remoras, or shark suckers, stay close to the underside of this bull shark off the Bahamas. These curious fish can attach themselves to their hosts by means of a sucker on top of the head; they feed on tiny parasites living on the shark's skin and sometimes catch other small fish that swim too close.

an unusual set of ripples or movements in the water. This will be detected by the shark, which will go to investigate. Not much is known about the sense of hearing in sharks, but it is likely to be linked to the sound-detecting sense, which registers vibrations in the water.

Around a shark's snout is a series of small pits. Though their exact function is not fully understood, they are thought to help detect minute electrical impulses given off by a potential prey species. This would be a very useful sense for a species living on the seabed in dark conditions. Further sensory pits are found all over the body of sharks, and these are thought to be similar to the tastebuds on the tongues of humans, helping to detect chemicals in the water.

Most people believe that sharks' appetites are enormous. In reality, they generally they take only what they require and do not gorge themselves. At one time it was thought that sharks could eat their own body weight in food every day. But studies of sharks in aquaria have shown that even if offered food continually, they will only consume about ten percent of their body weight in food in one week. Sharks can actually fast for quite long periods; if food becomes hard to find they are able to live off stored body fats and conserve energy by being less active. Those species that feed mainly on fish will also take carrion, which is why they are easily caught by anglers offering them dead bait, and they will also cannibalize their own kind if they come across another shark in difficulties.

Human divers are dwarfed alongside the vast whale shark. They are not in danger from this great creature, however, as it is a plankton feeder and has no interest in large prey. The whale shark is found mostly in the warmer waters of the Pacific Ocean.

A number of species of sharks are plankton feeders. They take only the smallest of organisms by a form of filter feeding. Some of these also happen to be the largest species of fish swimming in the sea. Basking sharks may reach 23 feet (6.9 meters) in length, although there are recent records of them reaching over 43 feet (13 meters). They feed by cruising slowly along near the surface, where plankton is most plentiful, and taking in seawater in their vast, gaping mouths. The water is strained through their sievelike gill rakers, and the plankton is trapped and swallowed.

During the summer months they can often be seen in calm conditions, swimming slowly along with the tip of the snout, the dorsal fin, and the tip of the tail all breaking the surface. In winter, when plankton is less plentiful, the sharks move into deeper water and cease feeding; the gill rakers are shed and will not grow again until the following spring, when plankton feeding resumes. An average whale shark will measure around 35 feet (10.6 meters) in length, while the record for the longest ever seen is 60 feet (18.2 meters).

Whale sharks are not only long, they are also massive in proportions, having unbelievably large mouths and very bulky bodies. These great fish are found in the warmer parts of the Atlantic, Pacific, and Indian Oceans and are not often seen. These sharks have ridged skin and are marked with spots of white and yellow. Like the basking shark, the whale shark has an extremely large liver, which acts as an aid to buoyancy. Basking sharks are sometimes caught for their liver oil, especially off the coasts of Ireland and Scotland, where their numbers are now declining.

Sharks eggs are fertilized internally after mating. The pelvic fins of the male are modified to form structures known as claspers, which are used to guide the sperm into the female's body. Mating is rarely witnessed by humans, but seems to involve the male twisting its body around the female. After fertilization the eggs remain inside the female to complete their development or are enclosed in a tough case and passed out of the body, leaving the young shark to develop inside a protective skin. Sometimes the empty egg cases are washed up on the shore after a storm—these are known as mermaids' purses. They are tough, leathery structures with tendrils at each end used to anchor the egg case to the seabed. Egg cases vary in size and shape among different species. The cases most commonly found are those belonging to the smaller dogfish and skates, but a 1-foot- (30.5-centimeter-) long egg case was once found in the Gulf of Mexico with an embryonic whale shark curled up inside.

Sharks produce relatively few eggs compared with most other fish. They are large eggs, however, richly supplied with yolk, which nourishes the developing embryo. When the young shark first emerges into the sea, either from an egg case or from its mother's body, it is quite large and strong and has a much better chance of survival than the young of most species of bony fish. Herrings produce millions of eggs in mass spawnings, and a very high proportion of these is eaten by a variety of predators. Those that do develop produce tiny fish, which themselves are eaten by predators in large quantities, so only a very tiny proportion of the original number of eggs will ever develop

Hammerhead sharks migrate in large schools up the Atlantic coast of North America in summer, but if the water temperature drops below 67 degrees F (19 degrees C) they disappear, preferring to hunt in warmer waters. They are long-distance travelers found in warm waters in many seas and oceans. A mature adult may reach a length of over 16.5 feet (5 meters).

The strange head of the hammerhead shark extends to form two flattened lobes on either side. The eyes are situated on the ends of these lobes, and the nostrils are close to them. This is thought to give the hammerhead a very accurate sense of perspective in both the senses of sight and smell, enabling it to quickly locate its prey.

A lemon shark rests quietly in shallow water near a tropical beach. Like other sharks, it can regenerate lost teeth—in as little as one week's time. This species has been known to penetrate large river mouths and can survive for a time in the brackish waters of estuaries.

The nurse shark spends much of the day lying motionlessly on the sandy seabed or in rocky gulleys, sometimes in large schools. It has an impressive array of teeth, enabling it to feed on fish. Although feared by some divers, it is not thought to be a threat, and there are no reliable records of attacks.

A shipwreck makes a good hiding place for a nurse shark during the day. It can rest here in safety and emerge to feed at night. A full-grown adult may reach a length of over 13 feet (3.9 meters) and has a very tough, protective skin.

The sand tiger shark can reach a length of 10 feet (3.1 meters) and is a fast-swimming, streamlined species of open water, usually found over sandy seabeds. This species spends its life continually swimming and can gulp air into its stomach to form a swim bladder to produce extra buoyancy in the water. It is an aggressive species, attacking anything that comes close.

into adult herrings. The sharks, on the other hand, produce fewer embryos of a larger size, which have a much greater chance of survival.

The eggs that are left to develop externally are provided with yolk to nourish the young, and those that remain inside the shark's body also have a yolk as a food supply. In some species, such as the mako and porbeagle, the developing young are known to eat other eggs inside the uterus once they have absorbed their own food supply. Some species form a type of umbilical cord and placenta, similar to that of mammals, so that the developing embryo can receive additional supplies of food from the mother. At one time, it was thought that they were related to mammals on account of this umbilical cord.

One shark above all is feared by man wherever it occurs. This is the great white shark, which is probably the world's largest carnivorous fish. Compared with the whale shark it is not so large, but an average great white will usually measure around 16.5 feet (5 meters) long. A 36-foot- (10.9-meter-) long great white was trapped in a fishing weir off New Brunswick, Canada, in the 1930s, but this was exceptional. However large it is, the great white is an unpredictable species and one that should be treated with respect. It is the species that accounts for most verified attacks on humans, but others such as the tiger shark, the mako, the whalers (not to be confused with the whale shark), and the hammerheads are all known to attack at times.

What provokes an attack is a matter for great conjecture. Is it sheer aggression, self-defense, or simply a taste for food? There are many recorded instances of shark attacks, and some analysis has been done of the circumstances. It is well known that sharks are attracted to blood in the water, so spear-fishermen who carry their catch around with them are especially at risk. The acute sense of smell of a shark enables it to detect and pinpoint the tiniest quantities of blood in the water and home in on it. Swimmers making splashy movements in the water, perhaps doing the crawl, are also likely to attract sharks, whereas those doing a more sedate breast stroke may go unnoticed. Bathers on a beach in shallow water where there is some wave action are probably not at risk from most sharks, but those diving into deeper water from a boat, especially if there has been some fishing going on, are at greater risk. Occasionally divers take liberties with sharks, approaching closely to photograph them or even tweaking their tails, so they should not be surprised if they are attacked.

Water temperature seems to be an important factor in shark attacks. At around 70 degrees F (21 degrees C), shark aggression increases critically. In equatorial regions, where the sea temperature is usually above 73 degrees F (23 degrees C), shark attacks can occur at any time of the year, but in cooler areas, attacks normally only take place during the summer months, when the sea temperature rises to the critical level. It is also during this time that most people take their holidays and go swimming in the sea. There are a few records of attacks taking place in colder waters.

The tiger shark of the Australian Great Barrier Reef is a large species, reaching a length of 16.5 feet (5 meters). Its blunt head and tiger markings help identify it, and its voracious feeding habits make it a much-feared predator. Females can give birth to between thirty and fifty live young at one time.

The bull shark, sometimes known as the whaler shark, is a fierce species that shows little fear of human divers. Although not deliberately aggressive toward humans, large specimens should be treated with respect. It earned its other name of "whaler" because it was often seen around the carcasses of freshly harpooned whales in bygone times.

The largest of all fish is the whale shark, a gentle giant that reaches lengths of up to 66 feet (20 meters). Although formidable in size and appearance, it feeds on nothing more than plankton, cruising slowly around near the surface, drawing water into its huge mouth, and filtering out tiny organisms.

Despite the small risk of attack by sharks, there is no excuse for persecuting them, for they are important predators and scavengers in the sea, performing a vital task by disposing of sickly or dead sea creatures. They show a perfect adaptation to life in the sea and should be left to swim unmolested. They have few natural enemies and seem to be immune to the diseases that affect other fish. The only real threat to sharks is the ignorance and prejudice of man. A recent and welcome trend among sea anglers has been to release sharks quickly once they have been caught and allow them to swim free. There is no need to kill every shark that is caught. Some people use "kill sticks" to attack sharks for sport. These are long sticks with an explosive cartridge at the tip, which detonates upon contact with the shark. This constitutes a particularly cruel and pointless act.

The eyes of this blue shark, like most other free-swimming species, are set on the side of its head, giving rather limited forward vision and restricting the view of what is immediately below its head. The size of its eyes reflects its nocturnal habits.

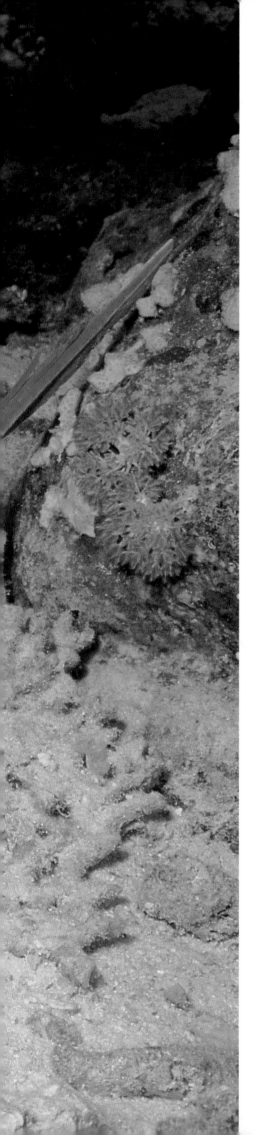

SKATES AND RAYS

Other monstrous creatures of unpleasing forms and formidable powers rove at will through these waters.

—P.H. Gosse, *The Ocean*, 1845

The skates and rays are members of the shark family that have flattened bodies. In most other respects they are the same, having the cartilaginous skeleton, the rough skin, the gill slits, and the habit of producing just a few large eggs. Their bodies are flattened from top to bottom so that they swim on their undersides—unlike some of the true flatfish, such as the halibut, which are flattened laterally and swim on the seabed on their sides.

Like the sharks, the skates and rays have a variety of feeding methods. Some are active predators, some feed by scavenging, and some are harmless plankton feeders. The flattened body form is an adaptation to life on the seabed and helps the fish to hide from predators or remain concealed until prey approaches closely. Some of the rays have adopted a free-swimming habit, however, and are more likely to be seen near the surface in the open sea.

Strikingly marked in black and white, the magnificent manta ray is a huge plankton feeder. It may measure up to 22 feet (6.6 meters) wide and weigh up to 3,000 pounds (1,350 kilograms). It cruises along just below the surface, with the tips of its "wings" just breaking through the waves from time to time. Projections of its head on either side of its mouth help sweep plankton into the mouth. Sometimes manta rays indulge in exciting displays of breaching, leaping clear of the

Stingrays are most abundant in warm coastal seas, and often occur in quite shallow water. This blue-spotted stingray is found off the coast of Egypt in the Red Sea. Like other stingrays, it bears a venomous spine near the base of the tail.

A clearnose skate, at rest on a sandy seabed, breathes by drawing in water through two openings on top of the head and pumping this over its gills. The water then leaves through the gill slits on the underside, avoiding the risk of clogging up its delicate structure with sand or mud.

Lampreys are curious close relatives of the true fish. Their mouths are ring shaped and armed with hooklike teeth, which help them grip on the flanks of a large fish and suck its body tissues. When they have taken their fill, they drop off and anchor themselves to stones while digesting the meal.

Some species of lamprey are migrants, spending part of their lives in the sea and then traveling up rivers to live in freshwater for a time before spawning. These lampreys are attacking a freshwater carp.

water, to the amazement of any onlookers. It was once feared as a "devil fish," but apart from the risk of its great bulk causing a small vessel to capsize, it poses very little threat to humans. It is a widespread species generally found in the warmer waters of the world's oceans.

Stingrays are able to produce an electric current in special cells located on their tails. This is mostly used as a form of defense against predators rather than a means of killing prey, as this is easily seized by the mouth. If a stingray is handled by an angler who picks it up by its tail, the resulting shock can be quite startling. Stingrays, in common with most other species, have excellent camouflage and are able to conceal themselves on the seabed simply by lying still. They can improve their camouflage by rippling the wings when they settle, causing a sprinkling of the bottom sediment to land on their backs, making them look even more like the seabed.

The thornback ray lives at depths of down to 1,650 feet (500 meters), feeding on crabs, clams, and small fish—caught easily on the seabed with its downward-pointing mouth. Mottled colorings on its back help hide it on gravelly backgrounds. If held in the air by its tail, a mature adult can give an electric shock!

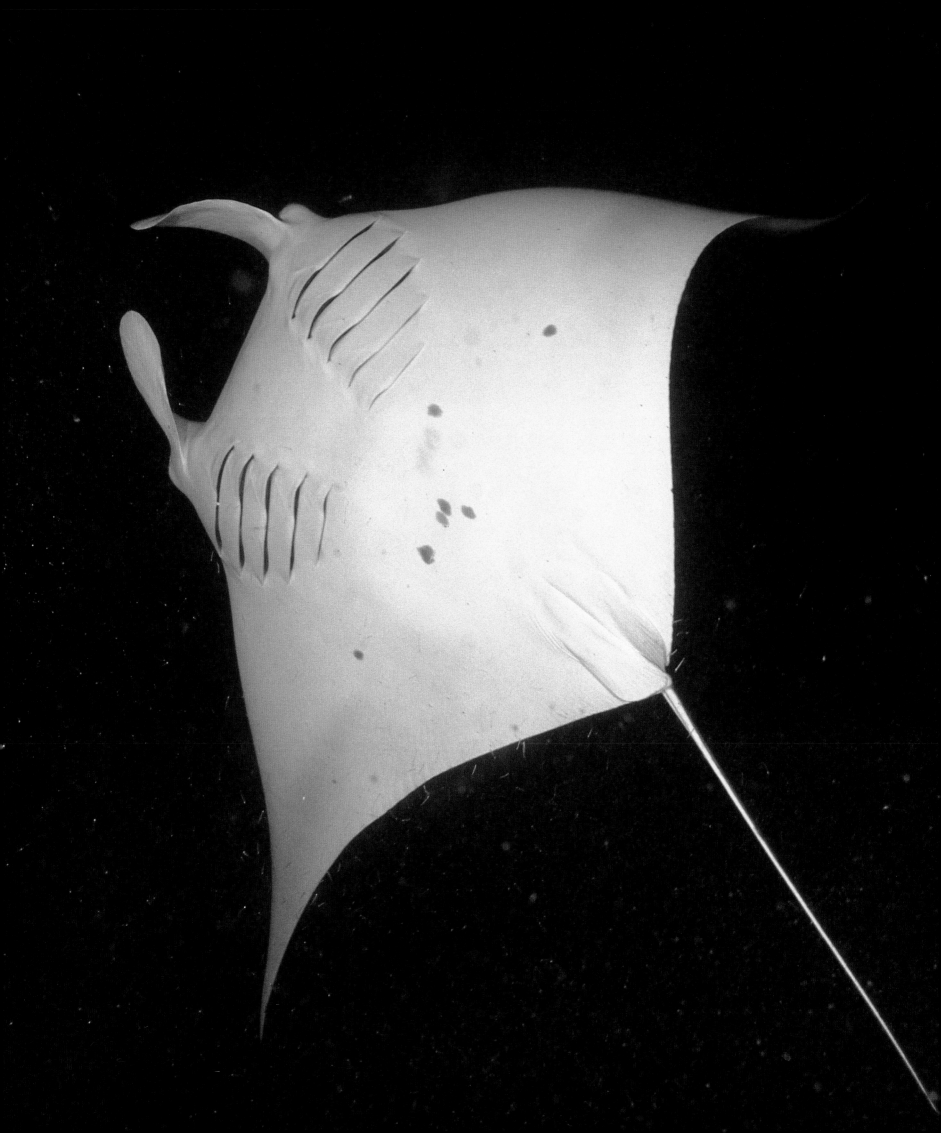

Manta rays are the largest of all rays, with a "wingspan" of about 23 feet (6.9 meters) in full-sized specimens. Although this is an enormous fish, it feeds only on the tiniest of creatures, taking mainly very small shrimp. Special netlike structures across the gill slits retain these tiny creatures as water is passed out.

A small school of eagle rays appears to fly through the water, propelled by graceful, winglike beats. This is a species of the upper levels of the sea, sometimes even breaking the surface in calm conditions.

The underside of the graceful manta ray shows its gill slits, through which water leaves after passing over the gills. The "horns" on either side help direct plankton and small fish into the mouth. Once feared and known as a "black devil," the manta ray is really a toothless plankton feeder and is not able to eat any large creatures at all.

Following page:

A southern stingray swims slowly over the seabed, showing its "wings," which enable to make graceful, gliding movements. Its mouth is hidden on the underside of its head.

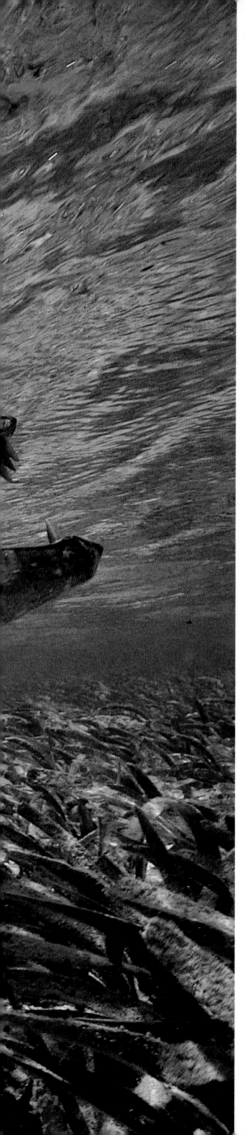

GIANT FISH

*An intelligent observer can scarcely fail to be struck with the perfect adaptation
of fishes for swift motion through a dense fluid.*

—P.H. Gosse, *The Ocean*, 1845

Tuna

The largest bony fish, that is, those with a skeleton composed of true bone and bodies covered with bony, disklike scales, are the tuna. The bluefin tuna can reach a length of up to 13 feet (3.9 meters), and the other tuna species are also quite large. Tuna are extremely fast swimmers, their highly streamlined and muscular bodies being perfectly adapted to life in the open ocean. As they swim, their fins are retracted into special grooves on the body to cut down on drag. Their powerful muscles are supplied with a red pigment called myoglobin, which increases the amount of oxygen available to the tissues during periods of intense activity. A tuna's body temperature is several degrees warmer than that of the surrounding water (which is unusual for fish), enabling the muscles to work even more efficiently. The blood system is designed so that the tissues conserve heat, making the fish's body considerably warmer than its surroundings.

Ocean Sunfish

The heaviest bony fish in the world is the bizarre ocean sunfish. From head to tail the average sunfish measures about 6.5 feet (2 meters), while from the tip of the dorsal fin to the end of the anal fin it measures about 8.2 feet (2.5 meters). This may not sound all that impressive when compared with a tuna or some of the sharks, but the sunfish is a bulky and rotund fish and may

The yellowfin tuna is an important commercial fish species, caught in large numbers in the Pacific. Tuna are large, perfectly streamlined fish, capable of swimming at high speed over great distances. They are voracious carnivores and eat large quantities of smaller fish like mackerel. They often inhabit the same waters as schools of dolphins, which also suffer at the hands of fishermen.

The powerful jaws and sharp teeth of a barracuda make short work of a mackerel. Nothing can escape once trapped between the jaws, making this a highly feared fish with few natural enemies.

weigh over 1 ton (.9 metric ton). Larger specimens are recorded, with reports of Australian sunfish over 10 feet (3.1 meters) long.

The sunfish earned its name from its habit of apparently basking at the surface of the sea in warm sunlight. It is probable that sunfish engaging in this behavior are sick or injured, for the real home of the sunfish is the deep ocean, where it feeds on much smaller fish and squid. The sunfish has an impressive, thick skin, rather like armor plating, which protects it from its few enemies. One further impressive piece of information about the ocean sunfish is the staggering number of eggs produced by a female; the ovaries contain as many as 300 million eggs.

One of the strangest of all fish, the ocean sunfish looks as if it were only half finished. It appears to be all head with no body or tail.

An Atlantic sailfish, hooked by an angler, is exhausted after a long fight and is drawn toward the fishing boat. The sailfish has a huge dorsal fin and elongated snout, which helps makes it a strong, very fast swimmer.

Marlin, Swordfish, and Sailfish

Marlin, swordfish, and sailfish are large fish of the open ocean that have long been sought by anglers because of the spirited way in which they fight when hooked. They all have a long, pointed upper jaw or bill, which is thought to be used to stun smaller prey fish. When hooked by an angler, the strong bill of the swordfish is sometimes driven into the hull of the boat. This is clearly done under the stress of struggling for its life, but there are accounts of wooden ships returning to port with the long bills of swordfish driven through thick wooden hulls, sometimes penetrating wood over 16 inches (40 centimeters) thick.

Both the marlin and the swordfish weigh as much as 1,000 pounds (450 kilograms) and reach lengths of 15 feet (4.5 meters). The 11.5-foot- (3.5-meter-) long sailfish is distinguished by its greatly enlarged, bright blue dorsal fin. This fish is a particular favorite among anglers because of the spectacular way it leaps out of the water when hooked. Sadly, there has been a decline in numbers of this species because of the interest shown in it by anglers, who mostly kill what they catch.

Barracudas

Barracudas are much smaller than marlin, swordfish, and sailfish, but still reach impressive lengths. They may grow as long as 6.5 feet (2 meters). What they lack in stature they more than compensate for in their formidable strength and fierce behavior. They are as feared in some areas as the much larger sharks. "Monsters of the deep" is a description sometimes applied to them, for they have been known to make attacks on human swimmers off the West Indies. Barracudas seem to be attracted by splashing in the water, which is why they often show an interest in human swimmers, and attacks are most frequent in murky water.

They have impressive, large jaws and sharp teeth and are also strong swimmers, capable of chasing and catching any species of fish they choose. The poisonous puffer and box fish, which barracudas often eat, taint their flesh, making them poisonous to any predator, including humans. This type of food poisoning has been reported several times in the West Indies.

The great barracuda may reach a length of over 10 feet (3.1 meters) and is a very strong fish. There are reports of attacks on human divers in the West Indies. Barracudas feed on a variety of smaller fish and are very fond of schooling fish like mackerel, which they consume in huge quantities.

The Pacific barracuda is a powerfully built, streamlined fish with a formidable array of teeth, and some can reach a length of 6.5 feet (2 meters). A feeding school of barracudas means trouble to any smaller fish that comes too close.

A jewel moray adopts an aggressive posture at the entrance to its hiding place in a coral reef. It may face competition for its home from other morays, as this can be a common species where the feeding is good.

Eels

Eels are members of the Anguilliformes order of fish. Most, including moray and conger eels, are marine dwellers. The typical male eel reaches 2 feet (61 centimeters) in length, while the female reaches 4 feet (1.2 meters).

Hiding in crevices in a coral reef or deep in a shipwreck, the moray eel remains out of sight until its prey comes close enough for it to seize with a rapid dash and a snap of the powerful jaws. The teeth of a moray eel are very impressive and capable of holding quite large prey. For this reason, it is thought of as a dangerously aggressive species. The moray eel is unlikely to launch an attack on humans unless strongly provoked. Its natural reaction to danger is to retreat deeper into its hiding place, but if divers approach too closely or corner a moray in a tight spot, they are likely to be fiercely bitten by the sharp teeth.

Exploring a reef at night could be very dangerous if morays are present, and there are several accounts of sailors having to beat a rapid retreat from lagoons when the morays decided to attack. When it is observed in the relaxed state at the entrance to its burrow, the moray appears to be panting and breathing deeply. Unlike free-swimming fish, which simply have to open their mouths as they swim along to take in water, the stationary moray must gulp in water all the time and pump it over its gills in order to obtain enough oxygen to breathe. When feeding, it cannot spend too much time chewing or breaking up food, as this would interfere with the circulation of water over the gills. Instead, it gulps down food very quickly, further enhancing its reputation as a fierce predator.

Some of the morays are most attractive fish sporting brilliant markings; these are called painted

Conger eels are plentiful in rocky areas or around shipwrecks, where they can find good hiding places and plenty of food. A 6.5-foot- (2-meter-) long adult is a fierce predator, eating any living or dead prey it can catch. Females produce up to seven million eggs at one spawning and then die.

morays. Morays were once thought of as a great delicacy, being a particular favorite of the Romans, who served them at banquets.

The conger eel is a much more camouflaged and dull-looking eel. It inhabits shipwrecks and holes in rocks and is most common in the Mediterranean, where it can be found down to depths of about 330 feet (100 meters). On average males measure about 3.3 feet (1 meter) in length and females reach up to 6.5 feet (2 meters), although 10-foot- (3.1-meter-) long specimens have been observed. The conger is a ravenous predator, taking any fish or crustaceans it can find, including a wide range of bottom-living and midwater fish, plus lobsters, crawfish, squid, and cuttlefish.

Congers reach breeding condition at any time from five to fifteen years, at which point the digestive organs degenerate and become useless, the teeth fall out, and most of the body is filled with the reproductive organs. The eels migrate to deeper water far out in the Atlantic, most of them ending up in the Sargasso Sea, where the eggs are laid. Each female can produce up to eight million eggs, and these hatch to form tiny larvae, which show little resemblance to the adult eel. After spawning, all the adult eels die. For about two years, the tiny larvae live a free-swimming existence in deep water, feeding on tiny creatures like shrimp.

When they reach about 6 inches (15.2 centimeters) long they develop a more eel-like shape and move nearer to the shore, where they adopt the habits of an adult conger eel. If a conger is able to find a secure hiding place, it remains there and attacks anything that tries to invade it.

Moray eels are most abundant on coral reefs, where they can hide in deep crevices. On emerging from its hiding place, the eel reveals it beautiful markings and coloration.

Large moray eels have a reputation for being aggressive and dangerous if provoked. Their mouths are armed with sharp teeth, and their strong jaws are ideal for crushing bones and shells. Lengths of up to 10 feet (3.1 meters) have been recorded, although most individuals do not achieve this.

Groupers

The groupers are large-mouthed fish found in both tropical and temperate seas, and some of them can grow to a considerable size. There are nearly four hundred species of groupers, and they exhibit a wide variety of colors and markings, but they all have the same basic body plan and general appearance. One striking feature is the very thick lips of the large mouth, which helps them catch and consume their prey; they are all carnivores and have been seen to take fish, crustaceans, squids, and octopuses. They are usually fairly sluggish in their movements, never wandering far from their territories on a reef or shipwreck. On the back they have two dorsal fins, and the first of these is armed with sharp spines.

Many groupers are hermaphrodites, simultaneously bearing male and female reproductive organs. A few start their lives as females, producing eggs when they are first mature, and then change into males as they grow older. One of the largest of the groupers is the Queensland grouper of Australia, which can reach a weight of 594 pounds (267 kilograms). The closely related jewfish of California is even larger, reaching a weight of over 770 pounds (346 kilograms).

Groupers are large, bony fish that live among rocks and in crevices, often near coral reefs. This tiger grouper has found a good territory on a shipwreck off the Florida Keys. It will not stray far from its usual feeding place.

The glum expression on this Nassau grouper is the result of its typically downturned and wide-lipped mouth. Powerful jaws help groupers crush shells and coral and devour the generally slow-moving prey they favor.

Groupers are normally solitary, swimming slowly around their territory and defending it against intrusions. Within each territory there are a number of hiding places, plus one or more principal holes to which the grouper retreats if danger threatens. Pictured is a beautifully colored spotted grouper.

Halibut

Some of the bony fish exhibit the bottom-living habits of the skates and rays, yet they accomplish this in a different way. The skates and rays are flattened from top to bottom, and when at rest on the seabed they are lying on their undersides. By contrast, the flatfish are compressed laterally and lie on their sides.

One of the largest of all flatfish is the halibut, which may reach a length of 13 feet (3.9 meters) and weigh as much as 660 pounds (297 kilograms). Sadly, the long years of overfishing and exploitation of this splendid fish have so reduced the numbers that these monsters are rarely seen now, and the average-sized halibut usually measures less than 6.5 feet (2 meters). Even so, this is still a very large and heavy fish compared with other flatfish. This giant fish lives on the seabed in depths of down to 6,600 feet (2,002 meters), where it feeds on other fish, especially cod, haddock, herring, and capelin. It also readily takes squid, octopus, crabs, and lobsters and grows larger and larger until reaching maturity, at around ten years of age.

Females grow faster than males and are mature at a length of 4.5 feet (1.3 meters), while males are mature at around 3.5 feet (1 meter). Spawning takes place in winter in fairly deep water, when the females release around two million small eggs. These are fertilized in the open sea by the males, and they hatch after about two weeks into tiny larvae, which drift

The enormous jewfish, sometimes weighing nearly 880 pounds (396 kilograms), has sandy markings that help it blend in with its surroundings. A fish of this size has few predators, but it is a slow swimmer and does not escape easily. A remora, or clingfish, has attached itself to its underside.

Flatfish such as the halibut are really lying on their sides on the seabed, in this case the left side. Although they start life as normal-shaped fish swimming in the open sea, they quickly migrate to the seabed and adopt the bottom-living habit.

As with this halibut, the left eye of a flatfish migrates around its head to lie on the right side near the right eye. As the fish is lying on its left side, the eye would be of no use in its original position. Halibut are long-lived fish, reaching an age of fifty years, by which time they may be 10 feet (3.1 meters) long and weigh over 440 pounds (198 kilograms).

along in the ocean currents. At first they do not resemble the adults, but when they are about 1.6 inches (4 centimeters) long they metamorphose into the more familiar flatfish and migrate to the seabed to continue their growth. This is a highly sought-after fish with an excellent flesh that is easily transported, so catches by fishing boats are high. Measures have been taken in recent years to conserve stocks, and the spawning grounds are now protected.

Anglerfish

One of the most extraordinary-looking fish of the seabed is the anglerfish. Seen from above it looks as if it is all head with no body, except for a tail and fins. It reaches lengths of 6.5 feet (2 meters). The anglerfish has a gruesome mouth, which only has to open wide in order for the angler to catch its prey. The mouth is so enormous that when it opens the volume of water rushing in draws an unfortunate fish in with it. In order to lure a small fish close enough for this method to work, the angler has a specially developed "fishing rod," formed from the first ray of its dorsal fin. This has a fleshy lobe of skin at its tip, and when wagged enticingly over the head, it attracts inquisitive small fish to their doom. Anglerfish prey mainly on small fish, but have also been known to take diving seabirds. The first insulin, used to treat people suffering from diabetes, was extracted from the pancreas of the anglerfish.

Sturgeons

The sturgeon is a primitive fish by comparison with the bony fish and is placed in a group of its own. There are about twenty-six species found in Russian or Asiatic waters, and they are of great economic importance to the people living along the rivers where sturgeon migrate to spawn. The sturgeon looks rather sharklike at first, but a closer examination shows it to have rays in its fins (as with bony fish) and five rows of bony plates running along the body. The tail is similar to a shark's tail, with the upper lobe being much larger than the lower one.

The sturgeon's mouth is very strange, as it bears no teeth, but can be extended like a short trunk. Just in front of the mouth is a row of four sensory barbels, which are used to help the sturgeon locate prey in murky water. Sturgeons live for most of their lives in the sea feeding on the bottom on small fish, worms, mollusks, and crustaceans. The long snout is used to root through the bottom sediment for the prey, which is then located with the barbels before being sucked into the tubular mouth.

Sturgeons can live to a great age and reach enormous dimensions. Specimens up to 20 feet (6 meters) long have been recorded; fish of this size weigh around 880 pounds (396 kilograms) and are approximately one hundred years old. It is very unlikely that a sturgeon of this size and age would be caught now, as pollution and overfishing have severely depleted the populations in most rivers where the sturgeon migrate to spawn. Females lay large numbers of eggs in gravelly rivers; some can produce over two million eggs at one spawning. The eggs hatch in a few days, and the small, emerging larvae feed in the river where they hatched for up to two years, after which time they migrate downstream to the sea.

The flesh of the sturgeon is very tasty and eaten in large quantities in Russia, but the greatest prize is the caviar, derived from the eggs of mature females. This highly expensive delicacy is exported all over the world from the rivers where the fish is still fairly common. Measures are being taken on some rivers to limit the size of the catch of sturgeons to ensure that this giant fish continues to thrive.

A mature male sturgeon may reach a length of 13 feet (3.9 meters), making it one of the largest of fishes, but most specimens only get to about 5 feet (1.5 meters) long before migrating from the sea up a freshwater river to spawn. Thousands are caught each year for their roe, which is processed into caviar. The "whiskers" are used to locate food on muddy riverbeds; sturgeons spend most of their lives in brackish waters where freshwater rivers meet the sea.

The strange shape and appearance of the anglerfish help it remain hidden on the seabed, unnoticed by its prey. The huge mouth stays closed until a tiny fish swims by. With lightning speed, the angler-fish then opens its mouth and gulps down the unfortunate victim. Large anglerfish can reach a length of about 6.5 feet (2 meters).

Following page:

A human diver comes face to face with a large sea bass near its favorite reef haunt. Despite its great size, the fish is unlikely to pose a threat to a diver who treats it with respect. Sadly, fish like this are considered prime targets for some spear-fishermen.

MARINE TURTLES

While pursuing our pleasant course amidst these sandy keys, we may often observe the green turtle swimming or floating at the surface.

—P.H. Gosse, *The Ocean*, 1845

Turtles are reptiles that have left the land and returned to the sea. Some may measure as long as 7 feet (2.1 meters). Their only contact with the land now is the time when they come ashore to lay their eggs. For a brief period they stay out of the water, but upon observation of them trying to haul their great bulk up a sandy beach, it becomes very clear that they are much more at home in the sea. Marine turtles have beautifully streamlined shells and long flippers to facilitate movement through the water. A swimming turtle appears to fly through the water, diving and turning with great agility, even though it has a rigid body. The lower part of the shell has a hingelike join, which allows the chest to expand and take in plenty of air to keep the turtle alive on long dives. The nostrils are positioned at the tip of the nose, so that when the turtle needs to breathe only the tiniest part of the body needs to break the surface.

At the start of the nesting season, turtles gather offshore from their traditional nesting beaches. Mating takes place in the water. The males are equipped with a claw on the front flippers to help grasp the females during copulation; their long tails also help in this process. Males swim up and down along the beach waiting for females to approach, and mating often takes place several times before a female can reach the beach.

Eventually the females have to make their laborious progress up the beach, hauling themselves forward with their front flippers and pushing with the hind flippers. Having reached the soft sand just above the

A green sea turtle off Maui, Hawaii, gets ready to surface for air after feeding on a reef. Turtles can remain below water for lengthy periods, but being reptiles, must take air into their lungs. The nostrils are at the tip of the snout, so only a tiny part of the body need break the surface when breathing.

The huge leatherback turtle, sometimes weighing in at around 1,430 pounds (643 kilograms), is very widespread, often venturing into colder waters than other turtles could tolerate. This female is excavating its nest in the sand of a Costa Rican beach before laying eggs.

A beach on Cephalonia, Greece, in the Mediterranean Sea, provides a nesting site for a female loggerhead turtle. Quiet beaches are hard to find in this popular holiday area, and the chances of the nest remaining undiscovered are slim. Some beaches are now protected to give the turtles a chance of survival.

The hawksbill turtle is a species found in shallow waters, especially near coral reefs. This brings it into contact with man, its most ruthless predator. Hawksbills sometimes feed on toxin-containing sea sponges; these do not harm the turtles but are stored in their tissues, rendering them toxic as well. Humans have been known to die from eating this poisoned flesh.

high-tide line, they excavate their nests, using only the hind flippers, and lay their round, white eggs. The digging process may take as long as an hour, with several stops to compress the sides of the pit with the flippers to prevent cave-ins.

Each female lays approximately one hundred eggs before refilling its hole to conceal the position of the nest. After this duty is performed the female makes a slow return to the sea, although the downward trail is far less strenuous than the climb up. The adult female turtle will then take no further interest in its young. The eggs, meanwhile, are safe in their nest, unless they happen to be on a beach where people are in the habit of collecting the eggs for food or where feral dogs and pigs can dig them out. If all goes well, the eggs hatch in a few weeks, warmed by the heat of the sun. The young turtles struggle to the surface of the sand and must then make the most hazardous journey of their lives and attempt to reach the sea. They have an instinctive ability to move in the direction of the sea and make their way rapidly down the beach toward the water. They have to run the gauntlet of crabs by night and seabirds by day, and once in the water face

Green sea turtles nest on beaches, usually coming ashore at night, when they are less likely to encounter predators. The lengthy process of crawling up the beach, excavating the nest, depositing the eggs, covering them, and then returning to the sea takes many hours, and turtles are often still present on beaches at sunrise.

further horrors in the form of sharks and other hungry fish.

Few survive this difficult time, but enough make it into deep water to perpetuate the species, and after many years of feeding and growing at sea, each turtle returns to the beach of its birth to complete the cycle.

Some marine turtles are herbivores, feeding on seaweeds and sea grasses, so they are confined to relatively shallow water where they can find sufficient food. Young green turtles are omnivorous when they first enter the sea, taking a mixture of plant and animal foods, but as they increase in size they switch to a diet of plant food. The hawksbill and loggerhead turtles are carnivores, feeding on fish, squid, and jellyfish. They cover great distances in the sea and dive deep in search of their food.

Turtles have few natural enemies once they reach full size. Many have been observed with parts of a flipper missing, quite likely the result of a shark attack, but apart from the risk from these large fish, the turtle's size and thick shell are excellent forms of protection. Both their speed in the water and diving ability enable them to escape from the attentions of most predators. The turtle's worst enemy is man. Thousands are killed every year for their shells and for a gelatinous material used in the production of turtle soup.

Although turtles are protected in some parts of the world, they are wide ranging and may be hunted in other parts of their range. There is a real danger of the total extinction of some species unless more stringent protection measures are applied. In common with so many other giants of the sea, the future of the turtles lies in our hands. We have identified the problem and know how to solve it. All we seem to lack at present is the will to achieve the best result.

After hatching, tiny loggerhead turtles unerringly make for the ocean. This is one of the most difficult journeys of their lives, for many predators try to catch them. Crabs and seabirds eat hundreds, but those that reach the safety of the waves stand a good chance of survival and will not return to the breeding beach for many years.

INDEX OF PHOTOGRAPHERS